BELLS &BIKES

ON THE TOUR DE FRANCE BIG RING
FOR YORKSHIRE AND ITS CHURCHES

This book is for my wife Sally and my son Thomas.
Encouraging and patient but very pleased
to see this thing finished.

BELLS &BIKES

ON THE TOUR DE FRANCE BIG RING
FOR YORKSHIRE AND ITS CHURCHES

ROD ISMAY

bellsandbikes.com

BELLS &BIKES

ROD ISMAY

First published in 2015 by Bells and Bikes.
bellsandbikes.com

A CIP catalogue record of this book is available from the British Library.

ISBN 978-1-909461-47-5 (Paperback)
ISBN 978-1-909461-48-2 (Ebook)

Design and production by Rod Harrison.
Vertebrate Publishing – www.v-publishing.co.uk

Bells and Bikes is committed to printing on paper from sustainable sources.

MIX
Paper from
responsible sources
FSC® C013056

Printed and bound in the UK by T.J. International Ltd, Padstow, Cornwall.

CONTENTS

CHAPTER 1

I AM NOT SIR BRADLEY WIGGINS BUT I'LL HAVE A GO

'Hello Rod, my name's Martin Green, a producer working with Welcome to Yorkshire. I'd like to include church bell-ringing in the opening ceremony of Le Tour de France and I'm told you're the man to sort it. I wondered if you might be able to give me a call.'

Thus began the final three weeks before the Grand Départ of Le Tour de France 2014 in Yorkshire.

The elite of world cycling was about to descend on God's Own County. Two hundred truckloads of inflatable hands, motorised Miffys, shrink-wrapped madeleine cakes and aerodynamic Haribo were about to be disgorged at Hull International Ferry Terminal and the church bells of the M1/A1 corridor were about to be scripted into the opening ceremony of the world's biggest annual sporting event.

It would have been more polite if I had actually answered the call. In the event, it was just another unidentified number on a mass of phones on a busy desk on a busy day. Meanwhile, I was totally absorbed in crafting an uplifting presentation for a bunch of accountants at the Post Office. A bunch of accountants? A balance of accountants? A peloton of accountants? Focus. Focus. Focus.

In fairness, the buzz had come from what I called my 'Tour de France phone', not my work phone, so I should have suspected something. It was probably going to be just another query about the race weekend though, so I waited for lunchtime before playing the message.

When I did finally hear it I gulped. I paused in shock and excitement. I tightened my tie and I checked the top button on my pin-striped shirt. In my mind I was crossing the finish line on the Champs-Élysées. I unravelled the strap on my office security pass and ensured the company logo was clearly visible to the imaginary phalanx of cameras in front of me.

For my team it was just another day. 'Oh yes, that's Rod in his spotty cycle shirt, on his way to the shower'. 'Oh yes, he's always on about the Tour.' 'Yes, that is indeed a folding bike under his desk.' Just another day. Well not any more.

This was the culmination of a long journey. It had been two years since I first became aware of Yorkshire's bid to host Le Tour, a revelation that had come to dominate my life outside of work ever since. It was also the culmination of twenty-five years as an ardent cycle tourer and as a Tour de France addict.

It was helpful that I had a kind of confessional box in our office. Team-mates Phil, Nigel, Peter and Lorraine, they took the brunt of it and they bore it well. Nigel even started cycling to work. Every day he would regale us with tales of the flies he'd consumed, the rain he had avoided and the goose muck he had not avoided.

Nigel was thriving on it. He was one of a growing band whose mountain bikes were now filling the staff bike shed. This was good news for the Cycle to Work campaign, even if it was a risk to staff satisfaction scores among the smokers as their standing space gradually dwindled under the handy rain cover of the bike store.

But hang on. Martin Green, master of ceremonies from the opening of the London 2012 Olympic Games is waiting for a call back.

'I am not Sir Bradley Wiggins, Olympic bell-ringer, but yes, I think I can arrange church bells for the opening ceremony of Le Tour.'

Brad, you absolutely nailed 2012.

2014, here come the bells of Yorkshire.

CHAPTER 2

CHANNEL 4 WAS RESPONSIBLE FOR MANY THINGS

There are many addictions, conditions and afflictions in this world. So many people seeking an escape from the reality of their own lives. So many people in pursuit of some brightly packaged, skilfully promoted salvation to their quest for a better sense of being.

Pro cycling, a test of fitness in the most beautiful scenery the world has to offer, has had its own dark corners of addiction and false prophets. Its combatants, men unsatisfied by the peak of physical condition, have resorted to dark potions to lift them ever higher to the podium. Their issues have, time and time again, taken the sport to the very brink of destruction.

For mere mortals like me, the issues began in the mid-1980s, with a behavioural spike for three weeks in July. The subliminal trigger was a multi-coloured number four on the TV screen at around 6.30pm and the recognised symptoms included an involuntary compulsion to recite the advertiser's mantra of 'Kronenbourg seize cent soixante quatre, sponsor du Tour de France'. To be even more specific, the condition was invoked by pressing the fourth button down on the right-hand side of the television set.

That, in itself, speaks of a better world doesn't it? The golden age of television, where the viewers physically involved themselves in sports programmes via a refreshing relay across the lounge. Marks for technical content could be earned as they elegantly lifted themselves from the sofa and lunged across the room in an aerodynamic form. Such exercise, minimising one's footsteps and maximising one's reach, could well have been the inspiration for Graham Obree as he reinvented bicycle design and rider posture in the 1990s.

Oh yes, those were the days of real television. None of today's viewer profiles, remote controls or channel-hoppers. Those were the days when switching channels and raising the volume to liberate the roars of the crowd on Alpe d'Huez required concerted physical effort. That was the hard school of TV.

That was where I cut my teeth. And that was the genesis of my personal addiction to Le Tour de France.

I can talk about it now. Oh, it holds no embarrassment any more. Wearing polka dots on ITV *Calendar* and BBC *Look North* is perfectly normal isn't it? Holding my shirt up in front of TV to take photos of Alan Titchmarsh or Harry Gration wearing my polka dots is not unusual is it? Oh yes, I have no qualms. Coming out; out I come; Hautacam. Le Tour, I can take it or leave it. I am, without doubt, in control.

Channel 4 was indeed responsible for many things, with Phil Liggett, Paul Sherwen and Gary Imlach becoming unexpected rivals to the Test Match Special team as sports commentators to whom you would like to send a cake. The late 1980s and 1990s would see them all find their cadence on the Granada Rentals Panasonic colour viewer in the corner of our lounge on Skinpit Lane, Hoylandswaine, overlooking Dodworth Colliery pitstack and Barnsley General Hospital. They went on to great things. Well, to be fair, they were already in a half decent place career wise. I, however, would get back on to the ripped foam saddle of my Triumph Tempest ten-speed drop-handlebar bike (with those extra absorbent sponge handle bar grips) and begin a run of sixteen years or so where I and my equally ill-equipped but naively keen cycling mates would ride the roads of the Tour, Giro and Vuelta in football shorts and golf shirts. The sight of my mate Edward, Young Geologist of the Year 1982, widening the gap, half a mile ahead on the N152 from Tours to Angers, wearing a slightly misshapen Sheffield Wednesday shirt, was just one of many iconic images of cycle touring before the Lycra boys, carbon kings and groupset gurus put cycle clothing on the catwalk.

Cycle touring, with my life stuffed in my panniers, with a budget for three thirty-six-shot film canisters, no digital editing, and maps to stare at in wonderment on tables in bars in places I could not pronounce … These were the things that, in potent combination with Channel 4, lured me into the sub-culture that is the addicts of Le Tour de France.

On the way, in hindsight, I realise I was taking photos of church bells wherever I went. This was the fertile soil from which bell-ringing for Le Tour de France in Yorkshire would naturally evolve.

What I would like to do in the rest of this book is to take you on an improbable journey of 'change ringing', cycling, community and culture. I shall start by taking you back a few months to a time when Yorkshire sat eighth in the gold medal tables at the Olympic Games, when fracking was not a word one would use lightly and when Le Tour de France started in rainy places like Rotterdam and Monaco.

Laissez l'histoire commence …

CHAPTER 3

AND YORKSHIRE WAS RESPONSIBLE
FOR MANY MORE

Yorkshire has always stood large on the world stage. It was home to the pioneers of club football, Sheffield FC (founded in 1857) and home to the first batsman to one hundred test centuries, Geoff Boycott (1977 in front of a home crowd at Headingley). Its chefs invented the Yorkshire pudding (220°F, hot oven and hot oil) and its armies were victors in the Wars of the Roses (1455–1487). At this point, I recognise that the historians amongst you, and the Lancastrians, may challenge my final observation there. The point is that Yorkshire did win seven battles to five on aggregate even if they were defeated in the final at Bosworth.

Despite this historical groundswell of success, there was some scepticism when Gary Verity (now Sir Gary, following the award of a knighthood), Chief Executive of Welcome to Yorkshire, announced that Yorkshire was bidding to host the 2016 Tour de France. Scotland had already put in a serious bid, apparently with backing from the UK government and British Cycling. Bit part players like Barcelona and Florence were also in the running.

It was, I suppose, a relatively strong field but when you are from Yorkshire anything and everything is possible. Vouloir c'est pouvoir as they say in Harrogate. Where there's a will there's a way. And there certainly was a will.

I found out about the plan on Twitter, in the summer of 2012. The bid had been under way for several months by then, but somehow in the excitement of life in accountancy, I must have missed the announcement.

I'd been a slow convert to the world of social media. I'd resisted mobile phones for a long time and Twitter, when I first heard about it, just seemed a time-consuming, frivolous chat tool. I was sure it had no place in my life and probably little merit for society in general. In a matter of days, however, its primacy as a medium of communications was clear to me and I had a rich, new source of high quality, timely news.

I went through the usual first steps of following celebs and then realising that their lives were desperately dull. Then, I searched with the hashtag #cycling and was soon in comfortable rapport with Les Vaches du Tour, a couple whose lives revolved around cows on the route of the Tour de France. It was these bovine bicycle fans who, on a cold and gloomy December morning, alerted me to the hottest news in cycling. 'Rod, you must be very excited,' they tweeted. 'Le Tour is starting in Yorkshire in 2014.'

Well, this really threw my day. I'd been merrily relaying the message to 'Back Le Bid,' but goodness me, was this true? Was Yorkshire really about to host Le Tour? And in 2014?

Some rapid googling confirmed that this was definitely not a rumour. Le Tour de France was indeed coming to Yorkshire and it wasn't going to wait for 2016. It would be here two years early.

The biggest event ever to take place in Yorkshire had just been unveiled to the world's media, and here was I, sitting at a desk in Derbyshire, being informed via Twitter by cow fans in Australia. A strange old world.

The essence of the story seemed to be that Paris was smitten with Yorkshire, local people were going to be invited to get involved on a scale never seen before in a Tour and, with strong community involvement, this would be the grandest Grand Départ ever.

This was far from a modest ambition. It was a devastatingly bold commitment. But it worked for me and, with a couple of ideas immediately taking shape, I would be happy to work for it.

CHAPTER 4

JANUARY 2013 – ENGAGING IN LE TOUR.
EARLY IDEAS

Le Tour de France is renowned for its majestic scenery, decorative tributes in farm fields and animated roadside crowds. It is the grandest among a rich array of cycle events, where the sport is played out on people's doorsteps and where, for free, whole communities find themselves in the same arena as their sporting heroes.

For my part I was blessed with two things with regard to the 2014 Tour; I worked for an organisation with hundreds of branches all along the race route, namely the Post Office, and I was a bell-ringer in an association which had dozens of churches overlooking the race.

These two things immediately gave me a conviction that I could help to prepare the arena for the race. I could see a great opportunity to deliver the best decorated and most helpful retail outlets on the race route and a chance for our church bells to ring out our most English of welcomes for the riders and fans from across the world.

Armed with these ideas I decided to call Welcome to Yorkshire to see what they thought about it all. I don't like cold calling but I had a strong belief in what I was doing, so I picked up the phone and took the plunge. When Tracy, in the Partnerships Team, answered my call I was among the very first business representatives to link in since the announcement that Yorkshire was to host Le Tour.

Ketul, a colleague at work, kindly rustled up a very compelling heat map of post offices in Yorkshire and this gave me a sound platform for my subsequent meeting with Tracy. Even though the exact race route had not yet been determined it was clear that the race would struggle to pass within shouting distance of less than a hundred branches.

This was great news. It was clear that post offices would indeed be able to offer valuable services to the huge crowds expected over the race weekend.

In fact, West Tanfield Post Office, just north of Ripon, would smash its annual records of ice cream sales in a single day. Reeth Post Office, potentially the most northerly postal access point in 111 years of Tour history, would develop a rash of red spots fit to attract the attention of TV helicopters from afar.

However, it was a small footnote on my agenda for the meeting that made an unexpected impact. It was unassuming 'Item 9' at the bottom of the page at that first meeting ... a mere aside ... church bell ringing.

It had seemed a little out of place with the other topics on the agenda. I had to reduce the font size to get it all on one side of A4, but it struck a chord. It resonated in that very first meeting. My challenge was to develop the idea into a credible and achievable plan. Little did I realise what a mountain lay ahead.

I might have been a bit irregular at ringing in the preceding few years, bedtime stories, London trains and PowerPoint had rather taken priority, but I knew who to approach and it felt like bells would be easy to do. I just needed to set my ideas out clearly on paper and get myself along to some meetings of bell-ringers. AGMs were looming and I needed to get Le Tour on to the agenda at the various gatherings across the county.

It was this that led me, to put my wellies on, load my rucksack with maps and embark on a somewhat hazardous hike over snow-clad pavements to Sheffield railway station.

I was going to get the train from Sheffield to Sandal and Agbrigg and, more specifically, to Sandal Magna church. I was going to unleash the idea of ringing for Le Tour de France on to the unsuspecting Central Branch AGM of the Yorkshire Association of Change Ringers.

The great thing about the stopping train from Sheffield to Sandal and Agbrigg was that it gave me plenty of time to type up a list of towns and villages on the route of Le Tour. In between the violent lurches of the slightly out-of-date rolling stock, I was able to match the communities to my guide of the church bells of Britain and come up with my first draft list of bells on Stages One and Two of the race route. It looked like there could be over forty of them. I could have been a bit on the high side in the cities as I couldn't tell what the exact route was, but York, for example, has eight bell-ringing churches and the race would surely pass with earshot of half of those.

Let's have a look at the list:

Leeds Cathedral	Askrigg	York St Martin's	Heptonstall
Leeds Minster	Aysgarth	York Minster	Mytholmroyd
Chapel Allerton	Grinton	York St Wilfrid's	Ripponden
Harewood	Middleham	Knaresborough	Elland
Otley	East Witton	Blubberhouses	Huddersfield
Ilkley	Masham	(Addingham again)	Armitage Bridge
Addingham	West Tanfield	Silsden	Holmfirth
Skipton	Ripon	Keighley	High Bradfield
Rylstone	Harrogate St W	Haworth	Sheffield Cathedral Anglican
Kettlewell	Harrogate St P	Oxenhope	Sheffield Cathedral Catholic

Knowing some of these churches myself, I was now able to make the next step in imagining what might be possible. Bells for the riders? Polka dot roofs for the helicopters? Lychgate interviews for the commentators? Vantage points for the cameras? This would surely excite the audience at the AGM.

First I had to find them though. Despite arriving in good time, I'd forgotten that it was necessary to walk round three sides of Sandal church to find the tower door. Then, part way up the stairs, I came to something akin to a tunnel where I had to carefully mind my head and try not to get distracted doing adventure films on my camera while a queue of slightly frustrated bell-ringers backed up behind me.

The church of Sandal Magna has a rich heritage, with its earliest building going back to the time of Edward the Confessor. Three subsequent buildings saw it through the turbulence of The Wars of The Roses, the Great Plague and even a readying of men across Wakefield to see off the Spanish Armada. The present church was founded in the sixteenth century. Its original four bells were augmented to six in 1812, and have been retuned during the subsequent two hundred years from F# to G.

The climb to the ringing chamber was, as I explained, pretty exciting. Once in it, the peal boards and rope displays on the walls presented a fascinating record of the story of bell-ringing in this corner of Yorkshire.

I joined a welcoming band in the ringing chamber. We rang the bells nicely before the meeting and the friendliness of the local ringers reinforced my conviction that Yorkshire bells and Yorkshire ringers could play a joyful part in welcoming Le Tour de France to our county.

The output of the meeting wouldn't be quite as fulfilling though. It wasn't that people didn't like the ideas. In fact, there was much respect for them. There was even a round of applause. The issue was that it all just seemed a bit remote to them.

'That all sounds great Rod. Very interesting ideas. But it's a long way off still isn't it. Can we deal with 2013 first?'

This would be the common theme at meeting after meeting. In hindsight it was a bit like 'don't call us, we'll call you,' but I didn't see it at the time.

It was a simple, and retrospectively understandable, disconnect between me, the Tour de France addict, and them, the people for whom Le Tour had not dominated their previous twenty years. The race was, quite simply, over 500 days away. It was not something they wanted to worry about yet.

In my mind, I was wanting to pin down a detailed action plan for who would do what in July 2014. They, however, were still recovering from Christmas 2012. They had all the challenges of booking holidays, buying clothes and sorting the supermarket deliveries for 2013, without needing to take on 2014 as well.

I get it now, but I was blinded at the time. I wanted a team to help me co-ordinate the ringing across the county, but no one was signing up. I wanted to have a plan for the eighteen months ahead, but no one wanted my actions yet.

I, therefore, sought comfort in the exploits of one of my Tour heroes. The Tour addicts among you will probably be familiar with Thomas Voeckler, leader of Team Europcar, and a famous veteran of two historic breakaways in Tours ten years apart. He spotted an opportunity, jumped from the main field and rode with little support for mile after mile in some of the hottest, toughest terrain you could imagine. In the face of adversity, he gained enormous time gaps, earned the coveted yellow jersey and held on to it as race leader for a further ten days each time.

His was a story of ambition, of endurance and of dogged stubbornness when none around believed the goal was possible. Arranging church bells for Le Tour often felt like this. The ringing community was in the hundreds, larger than the peloton of cyclists in a Grand Tour, but they all held back until the last minute, just like the sprinters' teams toying with a breakaway. It would be touch and go to the very final moments of the journey. There was no doubt that the ringers could pull out the stops if they wanted to, but they just didn't like to reply to emails or phone calls to say what they were actually planning in the build up.

Thankfully though, as with Thomas Voeckler, the 'crowd' kept me going. The ringers might have been reluctant to share their plans but Welcome to Yorkshire was loud in its support for bells and there were informal indications that the Tour organisation in Paris approved too. For an armchair addict of Le Tour, this was a very exciting time.

The project had to keep evolving though. Media interest created many unexpected twists and turns, but it was important not to lose sight of the original simple vision of ringing for the riders. The thing that became clearer and clearer though was the importance of a legacy. If we were indeed going to succeed in getting dozens of churches ringing for billions of fans on TV, we needed to capitalise on that interest to attract a new influx of would be campanologists to join us in the belfry.

You can judge for yourself how well we succeeded as you read the rest of this book. I hope, in fact, that it may encourage you to come and have a go yourself. You too could ring for a future Tour de Yorkshire. And if you don't live in Yorkshire then there is always the Tour of Britain in September each year. It would be a rare route indeed that failed to pass within earshot of a hundred or so churches with bells, given that there are over 5,000 ringing churches across the land.

Do let me know how you get on …

CHAPTER 5

BELL-RINGING –
WHERE HAVE ALL THE RINGERS GONE?

Church bell-ringing is in crisis. Some churches cannot afford to maintain their bells, some have good bells but no ringers, and some churches no longer have a congregation and are quite simply being sold for housing.

As regards 'the crisis', the doom mongers may be right or they may be wrong. Throughout this project, I certainly encountered some churches where there was no ringing at all, some where there was a complete dependency on the ringers from the next church down the road and some where the band was so small that you feared for the prospect of bells on Christmas morning.

To balance that though, I have to say how inspired I was by the vision and enthusiasm of some of the bands I spoke to – ringers at churches in busy cities and ringers at churches in remote villages with wonderful and romantic place names.

It was a mixed bag. But looking back this was one of the very things that connected bell-ringing and Welcome to Yorkshire at our first formal meeting focused purely on bells. Welcome to Yorkshire, voice of the county and globally recognised 'destination management organisation' wanted to help ensure church bell-ringing would thrive for future generations, for future Christmases and for future weddings where the brides and grooms were still mere twinkles in their parents' eyes. They relished the idea of bells heralding the cyclists along the route but also, without using the hackneyed word itself, they were looking beyond the race too, to the legacy for the county.

This truly was an unprecedented opportunity for a boost for bell-ringing and a chance in a lifetime to play our largest and loudest instruments for the biggest annual sporting event in the world.

The Central Council of Church Bell Ringers published a paper on the future of ringing in 2012. There was one overriding issue, an ageing profile of ringers with insufficient younger recruits coming in. Helpfully, there were several ideas to tackle it:

- A fresh focus on recruitment and retention
- Better encouragement of peer groups in ringing
- Incentives through local and national award schemes
- Support for ringing teachers
- Funding of equipment, including technology and training.

It was complemented by a presentation which you can watch for yourself on YouTube and, as if to prove that 'bells and bikes' was the new fashion, the presenter of this bell-ringing film was Ruth Eyles, British Cycling coach. Ruth was a new recruit to church bell-ringing only a year or so earlier. Have a look.

Ruth charted the very different demographics and trends for cycling and bell-ringing, cycling becoming ever more popular, for all ages, but bell-ringing becoming ever more skewed to the older end of the age spectrum. Hardly a launch pad for generational continuity.

Ruth wrote a great article in *The Ringing World* magazine in January 2014, entitled 'Better Basics Boost Beginners'. The premise of her article was that cycling and bell-ringing have a great similarity in their 'club' models, but that cycling reinvented itself by introducing shorter, simpler events (such as sportives) which gave entry-level cyclists stimulating, but less intimidating, challenges to help them progress in confidence and ability. Her conclusion was that where bell-ringers found 'simpler exercises to ring well' then it could significantly boost recruitment and retention.

I know that Ruth's article had its fans and its detractors. I am among the fans. I agree with her hypothesis and what I hope we showed in bell-ringing for Le Tour was that the public and would-be ringers lapped up 'simple ringing done well'. We were even able, through simple pieces, to do duets with musicians of the very highest levels as you will see in a later chapter. To an extent, it just depended on a positive mindset and a willingness to break the norm.

Like any form of music, very challenging pieces are possible and the ringing world has some very talented individuals who have really stretched the art of the possible in terms of complexity and endurance. Equally, some of the nicest bell-ringers have been dedicated to their art for decades but are content to remain ringing the simplest of pieces. I applaud them all. What I don't applaud are elitists who look down on anything other than perfection. And those people are not unique to bell-ringing. They exist in cycling too. They exist in all walks of life. Thankfully they can be avoided.

What I ask you, dear reader, is to come and have a go at bell-ringing and see if you might enjoy learning with us. To get to the point, if you don't, then please don't complain to me in 2040 when your son or daughter wants a church wedding and there's no one able to ring the bells as the happy couple emerge from the arched doorway into the sunlight and confetti and Uncle Kyle's karaoke fills the void that should have been bells.

When I kicked off this project to ring for Le Tour, I hadn't realised just what a state the future of ringing was in. I had started, purely as a Tour fan, seeking to celebrate the race in a very English way. The more I made my phone calls though, and the more the project ran, the clearer it became that this was a unique platform for changing the perception of ringing and the engagement in ringing. Very kindly, Gary Verity and his team at Welcome to Yorkshire wanted to support it too. Sadly, not all the 'grandees' of bell-ringing shared this vision, but thankfully, the grass roots local ringers did.

Now let me explain a little more about the origins of 'English Change Ringing' and one of the most popular 'methods' rung on church bells, a method happily called Yorkshire.

Bells are not unique to the British Isles, but change ringing largely is. Bells and similar musical instruments are used as a call to worship in many religions across the world, but only in England did bells gradually acquire full circle wheels and thereby enable the art of change ringing to develop. A small number of churches and secular sites in other countries now have such full wheel bells too, but the art largely remains English.

From Ron Johnston's *Bell-ringing: The English Art of Change-Ringing*:

> *'Bells are placed in church towers so that they can be used to call the faithful to divine service. Indeed it is part of the Canon Law of the established Church of England that every church should have one bell, and the Church's rubric requires an individual holding a service to 'cause a bell to be tolled thereunto a convenient time before he begin, that the people may come to hear God's Word, and to pray with him.' Originally this was because the great majority of the faithful would have only a rough idea of the time of day. At best, they would have access to a sundial, which is not always of use.'*

Bell-ringing, like other church music, has then developed through a combination of:

- Churches wanting the greatest impact in their music
- Bell-ringers (and musicians) wanting to excel and develop their art
- Competitiveness between bands in different churches, and
- Rich landowners indulging their interests and competitive spirit by donating substantial sums of money for better and better sets of bells.

Church bells, rung full circle on wheels, provide a unique form of music. Unlike most instruments where one can strike the same note several times in rapid succession, the music of bells is governed by the speed of rotation of the bell wheel. A musical form known as 'methods' has, therefore, arisen where bells strike in sequence through the octave and then gradually change places with one another in the sequence.

Taking the example of an eight-bell tower in the key of C, the bells when rung from highest note to lowest note would run down the scale as follows C B A G F E D C. You will often hear bells repeatedly running down the scale like that. Such ringing is called 'rounds', going round the scale.

The written notation for bell-ringing uses numbers instead of letters, and so C B A G F E D C would be written as 1 2 3 4 5 6 7 8.

Changes arise where adjacent bells in the sequence swap round. This may be done as 'call changes' where a member of the band, the 'conductor', calls specific pairs of bells to swap with each other. If, for example, the bells were ringing rounds and the conductor called '3 over 4' then the ringer on the third (number 3 bell) would hold up (slow his ringing a little) to pause and follow number 4 instead of number 2. The sequence 1 2 3 4 5 6 7 8 would become 1 2 4 3 5 6 7 8.

The alternative to 'call changes' is for all the members of the band to have learnt a 'method' such that they can all slow down or speed up their ringing to change the order of the bells in a specific pattern, such as shown at the end of this chapter in 'Yorkshire'. Here, each ringer learns the 'line' for their bell. At first glance it can look somewhat daunting, but on further review you will begin to see some structure to the pattern in that the bells move from the front of the order to the back, and vice versa, with particular zigzags (dodges) at particular points.

Yorkshire is, admittedly, a complex method, so here is a simpler method, 'plain hunt on 6'. The method can be represented by the 'diagram' on the left below or by the notation to its right.

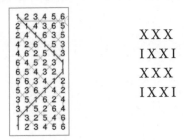

XXX

IXXI

XXX

IXXI

In this method, the first line of the 'diagram' shows the bells ringing rounds, then each subsequent line shows the effect of each change. In the first change, all three pairs of bells swap. In the second change, the bells at the front and back of the sequence stay at the front and back leaving just the four middle bells to do a pair of swaps. Then all three pairs swap and so on.

The county of Yorkshire was a thriving place for early bell-ringing, with one of the fathers of modern ringing, Jasper Snowdon, being born there. It is unclear whether he had any premonition of the Tour de France coming to Yorkshire, but he rang at Ilkley church and is buried there, just yards from the race route on the long westbound stretch up Wharfedale on Stage One. Jasper was a prolific ringer and writer, and the first president of the Yorkshire Association of Change Ringers.

A strong association grew from his work and its members composed many new methods. As a result the county is blessed with many ringing methods which bear the names of the towns and villages where the methods originated. In South Yorkshire, for example, there are methods for many places on the old trade routes into the Pennines such as Barnsley, Silkstone, Hoylandswaine, Cawthorne and Penistone.

One of the most popular methods is named after the county itself – Yorkshire Surprise Major, a method rung on eight bells. The diagram below shows the pattern by which the order of the bells changes, line by line during a course of Yorkshire.

$$(X38X14X58X16X12X38X14X78\text{-}12)$$

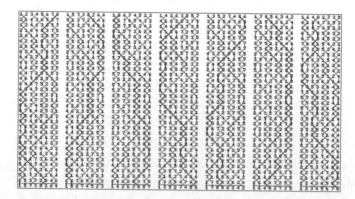

Church bell-ringing clearly had very strong credentials in Yorkshire. My challenge was to help our ringers understand the opportunities of Le Tour such that we could make our musical contribution to the grandest Grand Départ ever.

CHAPTER 6

PUBLIC VOTE FOR THE RACE ROUTE

When you think about the Tour de France, the usual questions that spring to mind are 'Where shall we go to see it?' and 'Where will we get the best view?'

Welcome to Yorkshire asked a different question. 'Tell us where the race should go,' said Gary Verity's team.

Rosedale Chimney perhaps? Ilkley Moor bahtat? The Wakefield rhubarb triangle? Dahn t'ginnel at end o' t'roooad? We were spoilt for choice. What a wonderful opportunity!

As a bell-ringer, I had some strong ideas regarding the best route – ideas based on fine architecture, local scenery, warmth of welcome from the locals and, of course, the richness of the bells.

Three towers in particular dominated my thinking: West Tanfield for the beauty of the church buildings, Penistone for the sound of its bells and Bradfield for its stunning setting on the edge of the Peak District. West Tanfield and Bradfield, of course, made it on to the race route. Penistone missed out on the peloton, but it got a decent consolation prize in bell-ringing terms as you'll see in a later chapter. That was a pretty satisfying outcome overall.

As a cyclist I had even more ideas, Holmfirth, Royd Moor, Strines. The tunnel of trees in Greno Woods on the approach to Sheffield. Barnsley Town Hall. This, in essence, was the core of my submission to Welcome to Yorkshire. My proposal for where the race and its twenty-kilometre long entourage should go.

To locals, these may strike a chord. To the Amaury Sports Organisation in Paris, the sound of them may have lacked the panache of Monaco, Biarritz or Harrogate. But then they didn't know how well woollen mills and steel works can scrub up with a splash of polka dots and a yellow bike. Nor did they know about Yorkshire bunting. Not yet. They soon would though.

For years my weekends had revolved around bell-ringing, church and then a bike ride to Holmfirth for a pint, a pie and *The Sunday Times* before the ascent of Holme Moss. A successful climb would be marked by a polystyrene cup of tea from the ice cream van in the windy car park, looking thirty miles north over Huddersfield to the peaks of Todmorden.

Back then, I lived in a little village called Hoylandswaine. There were many wonderful ways to cycle from Hoylandswaine to Holmfirth.

I could go in a straight line via the wind turbines of Royd Moor, imagining I was riding a cobbled spring classic past Dutch windmills as I bumped over the rutted tarmac above the snow line.

Alternatively, I could deviate to the north to pay homage to Denby Dale Pie Hall and its world renowned series of giant pies. The first such pie was baked in 1788 to celebrate the return to health of King George III and the most recent, to celebrate the turn of the millennium, was a twelve-tonne beauty escorted from oven to mouth by morris dancers around a six-axle flatbed articulated lorry.

If that didn't suffice, I could go slightly south to Stocksbridge, descending into the Valley of Steel with my brakes burning on the twenty-per-cent incline of Pea Royd Lane, home to the UK National Hill Climb Championships of 2014.

Or, I could set off in totally the opposite direction, bag a few climbs near the M1, take in a few million pounds worth of Henry Moore's finest work at the Yorkshire Sculpture Park off junction 38 before turning my pedals relentlessly towards a pint at The Fleece, 300 metres above sea level, in the foothills of Holme Moss.

Such a fine choice of routes; I love them all. But my favourite would start with a quick descent past conker trees to the sulphurous healing waters of Gunthwaite Spa, then a sharp climb past richly laden blackberry bushes up Cat Hill to the equestrian yard where once stood the vast pig swill silo of Pears' pig farm. After a couple of miles along the false flats of the A629, I would drop left on to the quiet roads of Royd Moor, getting my cadence to the rhythmic thump thump of the vast wind turbines on this Pennine equivalent of Table Mountain. The grand finale would be the dramatic revelations of the Holme Valley, Sid's Cafe, Woodhead Reservoir and, finally, Penistone Railway Viaduct.

These were places made for France 1 TV helicopters. These were places where I found my rhythm on twenty-eight teeth on my rear cog. These were places where I was big in spirit as I rode past the parked cars and saluted gaily clad picnickers with their flasks of tea and their Blue Riband chocolate wafers in small Tupperware containers. But at the same time, these were places where I felt my smallness too. I was a tiny dot of Lycra in a vast expanse of purple-heathered moors and skies stretching to distant lands with strange names like Rochdale and Lancashire.

I was pleased with the proposals that I tweeted back to Welcome to Yorkshire. My first foray into Tour de France campaigns, however, was all about a car. A mayor's car. The mayor of Barnsley's car. The car which had, in my opinion, the grandest registration plate there could ever be, 'THE 1'.

Back in the day, when five pence was a shilling, and when milk bottles had never heard of litres, vehicles registered in Barnsley all had HE in the number plate. The Yorkshire Traction buses were HE, the fire engines were HE and the mayor was top of the tree, the big 'THE'.

I imagined that registration plate shining proudly on the lead out car for the race. I imagined Bernard Hinault, five times Tour Champion, waving the flag for France in 'THE 1'. The *Barnsley Chronicle* retweeted my idea, the deputy mayor 'favourited' it and grandad Barry told of how he sold 'THE 2' second-hand from Eyre Brothers motor dealership on Regent Street a third of a century earlier.

'THE 1' is a bit like *Doctor Who*. It has had several reincarnations, just as Barnsley has had many regenerations. Strange, varied, beautiful guises over the decades. The car. And t'town.

In 2003, Will Alsop, an architect inspired by Italy, proposed a vision for the re-modelling of Barnsley as a Tuscan hill village. The plans dominated The *Barnsley Chronicle* for weeks and they continue to make a fascinating display in the Barnsley Museum in the former Town Hall right now. But 'THE 1' was not to be infected by Italian-ness.

Perhaps, if we host the Giro d'Italia bike race one day, it might show us a bit of Fiat. But 'THE 1' remained staunchly British until latterly, like a temporal aberration of a Bond car, the inevitable happened and three other letters appeared outside the Town Hall. BMW.

But, Christmas was upon us. A bitter winter set in and in January the Tour route was announced, without Barnsley on it.

The mayor's car didn't, therefore, make it into the caravan of Le Tour. However, we don't give up that easily in Barnsley. The Mayor's Parade moved forward from its usual date in July to Saturday 14 June. The branding was 'all things French' and 'THE 1' led an early fanfare for the final twenty-one-day countdown to Le Tour.

A few people moaned on the internet that 'THE 1' should be sold to reduce council tax. A good few proud locals told them where to go. It would knock pennies off each house's tax but rob the borough of one of its most iconic brands.

And so, while 'THE 1' didn't get into the race itself, some of the roads that I suggested did. Some others came to fruition in the inaugural Tour de Yorkshire a year later in May 2015, and by the time you read this, who knows where the bikes will have raced since.

I travel some of the roads today, on journeys the same as I did in years before, but now I pay homage to the brown Tour de France signs as I go. My heart pounds, I have a resurgence of pride and a thought that this is where Vincenzo Nibali catapulted himself into the Maillot Jaune. This tarmac. These traffic cones. These are the monuments to Le Tour. We salute you.

But there is more. What the world would eventually come to see in the race on Saturday 5 July and Sunday 6 July 2014 was not just the beauty of the Yorkshire scenery. What they saw was a community, a spirit, a warmth of welcome and mile after mile of crowds, the likes of which have never been seen outside of Paris or away from the twenty-one hairpin bends of l'Alpe d'Huez.

The roads that Yorkshire voted for, and which the ASO took up, combined the very best of country and community. They also came past some rather splendid churches. I'd encourage you to try some of those roads. Try the bells too. I think you'll like them. The roads and the bells.

CHAPTER 7

HOW TO GET SPOTTED AT A TOUR ROADSHOW

In the spring of 2013, Welcome to Yorkshire launched a series of roadshows across the county to help 'inform and educate residents, businesses and communities about the history of the Tour de France.' The attendees ranged from ardent club cyclists to pub landlords and from chief executives to ukulele bands.

I thought I knew enough about the history of the race but I was very keen to attend one of these roadshows to find out more about the local organisers' plans and to see what other community groups were up to. I also had a vain ambition that some worthy local business might want to sponsor an event at a church during a bell-ringing tower open day.

There was a long list of dates to choose from but they all seemed to clash with something or other that was mission critical at work. One particular date, however, hung pleadingly in my calendar; Thursday 9 May at Sheffield Town Hall starting at 10am.

10 a.m. ... 10 a.m. ... This was clearly not perfect timing when I was supposed to be in an all-day meeting in London. Even if the Government had got on with spending £20 billion on HS2 and slashing the journey time from Sheffield to London by an oft-quoted seven minutes, I couldn't have made it. Those seven minutes might make all the difference between the Maillot Jaune and short-lived podium fame on the second step on the Champs-Élysées, but it wasn't going to get me from the Tour roadshow in Sheffield to the meeting with the finance director in EC1.

But then, at the last minute, well 10pm the night before, it came to me. A moment of brilliance, sheer genius, awesome innovative thinking, namely to use the phone. This was truly ground-breaking stuff. Save the train fare, facilitate the school run and deploy leading edge agile working practices. I could also avoid the awkwardness of when to propose a loo break during intense analysis of strategic projections and hurdle rates on transformational change investment programmes. I would phone in.

Tracy got my 10pm text message and within moments had confirmed a space at the Roadshow. A contented night followed and as the big day dawned, I pushed my Debenhams machine washable suit to the back of the wardrobe and donned my 1992 Tour de France King of the Mountains polka dot shirt for the first time on my Tour PR campaign.

Later that same morning I would find myself at Sheffield Town Hall in a room full of suits. Even cyclists in suits. This was one thing I never understood, why wouldn't you wear polka dots to a Tour meeting?

I'm not a natural room-worker, a mover or shaker. Not someone who relishes walking into a full bar and attempting to engage in conversation with a bunch of nice folk who've already found someone to talk to and don't need me interrupting them. However, in polka dots, everyone needs interrupting. With these red spots, this cloak of invincibility, there ain't no mountain high enough to stop the seamless integration into the network of the room.

This was a game-changer and no matter how many times I deployed it, it was as effective and fresh as ever. When I say fresh, I have to admit that the shirt had been hand-washed with shower gel innumerable times on hot Alpine and Pyrenean climbing days, before being air dried on the back of my panniers, diverting onlookers attention from the Y-fronts clipped under my rear brake cable as it ran along the top tube of my bike.

A bicycle is blessed with no end of innovative fixing points for drying washing. Especially if you deploy excessively large panniers front and back. Peter, my best man and touring companion from Dublin to the Dolomites, regularly reminds me of the day my washing cost him his most promising chat up yet with two pretty German tourers on the climb to Voss in Norway. He had kindly helped them with a puncture when I trolled up with Y-fronts and grimy socks drying on each pannier. It was evidently not the lederhosen of choice in their homeland and quicker than we could say frühstück, they were gone. Lost, yet immortalised. Forever to be remembered as the opportunity at a puncture, where the dream was popped by pants.

I cycled to the roadshow. I didn't have any underwear drying on my frame. The spots sufficed. I arrived early. Keen to recover ground after my awkwardly late request for a seat. There would obviously be lots of cyclists. Obviously lots of bikes to lock up before the meeting. Another reason to get there early. To get a space.

'Er, I'm here for the Tour Roadshow upstairs, is there bike parking?'

'Oi, Stan, there's a bloke here sez he wants to park his bike. Summat about a cycling meeting. He's not staff. Tha' gotny ideas?'

I squeezed against the window of the security desk. Squashed in to allow the Cycle to Work members of the Town Hall staff to push past to what evidently was a nice internal lock up for bikes.

This was most encouraging. Cycle Sheffield should be pleased with the great work they are doing to encourage safe cycling to work in what many, wrongly, write off too early as a cycling city simply because of its hills. Come on, it's the hills that make it.

This was good news – cyclists. Perhaps they were going to the roadshow too. Perhaps Bernard Hinault would be here? Ten minutes passed by though and Stan had no solutions. 'What's this gig he's at? Summat about cycling. Nar he'll have to lock up outside somewhere.'

And so it came to pass that not only was I the only attendee in spots. I was almost the only person on a bike. Except praise be for Mick from Cycle Sheffield. It was a pleasure to meet him at last after much help over my inept saga of making a £3 bank transfer payment to join Cycle Sheffield. Mick and his fellow campaigners were doing a great job of promoting urban cycling and in time would inspire the cyclists of Sheffield to turn Herries Road from a grey urban climb on the last few miles of Stage Two into a brilliantly yellow bunting paradise from which Nibali would plot his final break.

I legged it up Division Street for the second 'Praise Be'. This time thank you to Rehab Bikes with their £1 secure lock up for the day. With maintenance services available, this was and is a great facility for urban cycle commuters without office bike parking. Nice one chaps.

I now had a suitably alpine sweat on by the time I got back to the Town Hall. The polka dot shirt was in proper race shape.

Numerous dignitaries were in attendance and many statesmen of the northern cycling scene. Unwittingly I sat with Gian Bohan, owner of Nonna's and soon to be central figure in Eroica Brittania, the handsome cycling event now becoming a firm fixture in the European Cycling Calendar in the heart of the Peak District. Choir leaders were there, brass band conductors relished the opportunities ahead and local organic seed producers made a compelling pitch for Sheffield-grown yellow flowers.

Phil Jones of Sheffield Hallam University set the scene for what would become powerful student engagement in Le Tour. And I got two minutes on Radio Sheffield drive time courtesy of Andy Kershaw, whose eagle eyes spotted my polka dots as a potential cyclist among the suits.

I was there with two hats on, so to speak, I explained. Representing hundreds of post offices on the route and dozens of church bell towers. What the listeners must have thought I don't know, but my in-laws enjoyed the interview in farthest Sussex, courtesy of iPlayer. Perhaps a career in media beckoned? Maybe not. Stick to the washing.

By the time I attended my second roadshow, four months later, a lot had happened and a lot had become clearer. From a Tour point of view, the route was increasingly well-publicised and most communities now had clear advocates in their midst – people perhaps lacking formal working parties or PR strategies yet, but passionate and vocal individuals who would stoke the fires of social media. So much so that during the 100th edition of the Tour, a year before the race was to come to our fine county, Paris would have to ask Yorkshire to tone it down a bit until the baton firmly passed at the end of July.

Yes, in that landmark year for Le Tour, a year that would see iconic imagery of speedboats off Corsica, Froome in yellow and a laser show on the Arc de Triomphe, it was Yorkshire who were top of the Google hits. We were loud and we were very French. Le Tour had its new home, we would do Christian Prudhomme proud. The vineyards of Holmfirth and the breweries of Cragg Vale would flow sweetly.

The Yorkshire Festival, 100 days of arts and culture to precede Le Tour, had also been announced. This was to be the first such cultural festival before a Grand Départ. It would gain significant backing from The Arts Council and from local business, particularly Yorkshire Water, the largest landowner on the race route. Our reservoirs would be a match for the bays of Corsica.

From a bell-ringing point of view, I knew where the towers were and I had begun telephone calls to them. There was broad recognition that it would be good to ring to welcome Le Tour. But there was also a certain lack of urgency. In my mind the Tour was nearly here, there was after all only twelve months to go. I was already on the case after midnight on an almost daily basis, but my contacts in each church just didn't seem to share my sense of urgency.

Now I see it. I look back fondly on those voicemails which got no reply, the request that I stop texting so and so, those letters with no response. There were two things in hindsight:

1. It's the hard world of sales; a ten per cent response rate is good, not bad
2. A year away does actually mean a whole year away.

Maybe I had been a bit early out of the blocks? Maybe it would indeed be polite to at least let the preceding Tour de France run its course first.

The thing was though, bells had been taken up by Welcome to Yorkshire now. I was beginning to see the press cuttings of Tour roadshows 100 miles away where church bell-ringing was being talked of as a key feature of Yorkshire's welcome to Le Tour. I dug. I searched. It turned out to be echoes of my own suggestions at the Sheffield roadshow, four months earlier, reverberating around the county.

I should confess at this point that I did, at several times over the next year, wake up with a slight panic. Will anyone actually ring a bell? Will they all be put off by the scaremongering about road closures? Have I, a recently infrequent ringer, got myself out of my depth in commitments to the world's greatest bike race? What on earth have I done?

There's a condition called Imposter Syndrome – it's when you are sitting in the middle of a really important event, leading the debate, and suddenly decide you are wholly unqualified, unsuitable, unjustified to be there. Not many people admit it publicly, but many have it. I did, big style. Nevertheless, I confronted my demons and set out my hit list of ideas for Le Tour, tackling 'head on' the question from towers en route of 'what's in it for us?' And thus began the not insignificant exercise of collating, issuing and following up 'Tower Briefings' to ringers along the route, from an incomplete address book and no email list.

Looking back, it must have answered the question fairly well because we made a lot of the ideas come true. Carry on reading and I'll explain how …

CHAPTER 8

MAY 2013 –
BRADFIELD FESTIVAL OF MUSIC AND THE UNFINISHED SYMPHONY

There are arguably three pivotal events in the calendar of world music. Firstly, there is Glastonbury, secondly, The Last Night of The Proms and, finally, The Bradfield Festival of Music. Bradfield Festival is a week-long programme of nationally recognised artists and local amateur groups. It gives a magnificent platform for young musicians to perform in public and, with concerts in the Parish Church of St Nicholas, it offered the potential for some Tour de France bell-ringing. Bradfield, of course, was right on the route of Stage Two, The Steel Stage. My idea was that we would perform a world premiere of a previously unrung method, during the festival, and dedicate it to Le Tour.

Bradfield sits on the edge of the Peak District National Park. The village is split in two by a nice sharp hill. High Bradfield, with its ancient church of St Nicholas, sits proudly on the steep south-facing slope. It calls out to passing TV helicopters to zoom in on its intricate buildings, its wandering livestock, its drystone walls and its thirsty cyclists. Low Bradfield nestles on the valley floor, full of happy walkers eating Our Cow Molly ice cream from the village post office as they pace the lush green outfield of the cricket pitch, working up an appetite for a second ice.

The village is a favourite with cyclists. It is a scenic half-hour or three-hour ride from Sheffield, depending on ability and café stops and it is the gateway to the raw 'Dolomite-sharp' slopes of the Strines country road. Moreover, it now has some of the country's, if not the world's, smoothest, blackest tarmac. This is the Majorca of Sheffield, the cycle training Mecca of the city. Bradfield also has eight church bells. These are in the key of F. What better place to ring out for Le Tour?

Change ringing, as you may remember, involves ringing bells in ever-changing sequences as governed by diagrams. There are no end of different sequences which can be rung and, if you happen to be the pioneers who are the first to ring a particular sequence for a minimum number of changes, then you earn the right to give this 'method' a name of your choice.

My friends in the Barnsley and District Society of Change Ringers and I had rung new methods ourselves in the 20th and 21st centuries. The most glorious, in my experience, being in May 1997, the month Barnsley rocked to 'It's Just Like Watching Brazil' after Danny Wilson led Barnsley Football Club, The Tykes, to the Premiership for the first time in their history. Brian, our captain and conductor, chose a suitable composition from the book of unnamed methods, we wound our way up the spiral stairs of Barnsley St Mary's church, and forty-eight minutes later 'Oakwell Delight Minor' was announced to the world.

Now, had anyone ever rung an unnamed method at a church tower on the race route of Le Tour de France? Had anyone even done English change ringing for Le Tour before? This obviously needed secrecy. No one must know. No one must beat us to it.

In hindsight, I may have over-exaggerated to myself the risk of someone else trying to dedicate an unnamed bell-ringing method to a bike race. No one has yet said they know of any competitors trying to get there first. They may be being gentle with me though. They may think that the truth will hurt me.

Nevertheless, the plans rolled on and, like a conjunction of the planets, three things came together all of sudden. The Yorkshire media were increasingly talking up Le Tour as the 2013 race approached, Philip Charles-worth (recognised originator and conductor of unnamed methods) had a special method in mind, and it would soon be the Bradfield Festival, featuring a choral concert with the Bishop at St Nicholas church. The die was cast.

I arrived early, intending a quick visit into Bradfield Post Office before-hand to share Tour notes with Heather, the Postmaster, but here came setback one; she was out. However, that did not dampen my enthusiasm nor stop me spending fifteen minutes taking photos of my polka dot shirt on a gate-post in front of the church. There was no mobile reception so I was unable to tweet them, but it was a very fruitful session nonetheless. It gave me my new and enduring social media logo. The fact it promoted a certain French supermarket sponsor of Le Tour from twenty years earlier, not the current supermarket sponsor, passed me by. This day was about bells, not brands.

We rang. We pealed out over the village. The pub car park was alive with the sound of music. Crash clang. We went wrong. I confess, it was probably me. We restarted. We went wrong. We re-started again. We went wrong again. The bishop approached. The choir were seated. Like the backmarkers on a mountain stage we were out of time. We weren't disqualified as such. We simply failed. The PR splash into the 2013 Tour slipped by.

Summer came and Chris Froome won the 100th edition of Le Tour. Barnsley narrowly missed relegation following a 2-2 draw with Huddersfield Town on the final day of the season and the new tarmac continued to flow like wine. Every road closure, every traffic island removal, every cone, every resident's parking notice about towing cars away, all these things heralded a better world. A world post potholes, a world of roads smoother than the green baize at The Crucible, a world of bunting … a world of bells and bikes.

Winter passed with no snow. Jools Holland welcomed us into 2014. The Yorkshire Festival Programme was launched to the world and before we knew it the festival itself was commencing. What better moment to finish what we had started in 2013. Surely this was our time. I telephoned the band and happily we had six willing ringers. Then suddenly, two were unavailable. Within days two more had a late notice clash. One returned though and three more were soon found. We had a new band; a new dawn.

Unburdened by baggage from the failure of 2013, the anticipation grew. At least it did for me. Nevertheless there was still time to get distracted. Bradfield churchyard is renowned for its resident sheep who, being protective of their space, like to leave lots of little markers to deter invaders. I looked hard, swung my foot like a pendulum and created a space between the droppings before lying down. Snap snap. Never ever go bell-ringing at a church on the Tour route without taking photos of your polka dot shirt. Holding it at a respectful distance from the graves I captured the red spots, framed with vibrant spring daffodils, the yellow jerseys of the flower kingdom. The church tower loomed large over the scene.

Trevor gave me a knowing look. 'Rodders ... ' Brian glanced at me with one of those expressions that makes you wonder if you are properly focused on the job in hand. The other ringers, unburdened with cameras or sheep droppings or spotty shirts, swaggered nonchalantly to the belfry stairs. And in the background there were French voices. French voices? Yes, French voices. I was thrown.

I knew we needed to start ringing in five minutes time but that could be Bernard Hinault over there. It could be Thomas Voeckler. It could be Louis XIV. Whoever it was they were French and they were not getting away on a landmark date like this.

'Nous sonnons les cloches pour Le Tour,' I said. 'Bienvenue Le Tour. Il y a beacoup d'églises et beaucoup de cloches près du route du Tour.'

'C'est un premier mondiale. Lisez l'hebdomadaire le semaine prochaine,' j'ai dit.

Whether they had any idea what I was on about, who knows? Will they be reading this book now? If you are, if you are the two Frenchmen studying at the University of Sheffield, please may I say 'Bonjour encore une fois.' You had enjoyed a great day walking in the moors around Bradfield. And you had just made my day. This was surely an omen. A positive omen of Frenchness for our ringing.

Malheureusement we went wrong again. Between us, and respecting the anonymity of my co-conspirators, Ringer A hadn't expected to be placed on that bell, Ringer B made me laugh too much, Ringers C and D did their utmost in the face of adversity and Ringer E hadn't had his tea despite the rich blessings of time that retirement can bring. To cap it all, and as one ringer (let's call him Brian) had feared, I hadn't learnt the method well enough. This was not a maillot jaune performance.

We didn't get our quarter peal. We didn't strike that magical minimum number of changes to qualify to give a proper name to this 'unnamed method'. We didn't get to dedicate a ringing performance to Le Tour de France. This was the one that got away. On the plus side, it was a nice pint afterwards in The Old Horns Inn next door and there was a very nice Tour Yorkshire shirt draped over the bar inviting photographs. But the bell-ringing eluded us.

Many other things would come to pass. Ringing would get more than its fair share of airtime. Much would be looked back on with happiness and pride. But this was the one that got away. This was the unfinished symphony. My only hope, Messieurs Prudhomme, Hinault et Verity, if you are reading this, is that you may bring Le Tour to Yorkshire again. And then, when you do, nous avons l'intention d'essayer harder next time.

CHAPTER 9

AUGUST 2013 – RECCE THE ROUTE.
BUSINESS AND BELLS AND BIKES

Eight months had now elapsed since Yorkshire unveiled its plan for the grandest Grand Départ in Tour history. In that period I had campaigned extensively among churches and retailers, I had spectacularly failed to deliver a world premiere bell-ringing performance for Le Tour and I had bought more new Ordnance Survey maps than might be expected in a world of Garmin and TomTom satnav. What I had not done was to spend much time actually on the race route.

During our summer 2013 holiday in Wales, accompanied by my maps of Yorkshire, I decided to remedy this. I telephoned Reeth Post Office in the Dales and made a plan for a long day visiting churches, tourist offices and postal outlets on the roads of Stage Two of Le Tour. My plan was to improve my knowledge on the ground, build a network face-to-face and get some commitments for the year ahead.

Martin at Reeth Post Office was, as it happened, a keen local cyclist. He also presented at drive time on Radio Teesdale. His village shop, on the green in Reeth, was grandly located at the head of the long run down to Harrogate on Stage One of the 2014 Tour. This was a perfect place to share ideas and build plans.

A year later, when the race finally came to town, the pace would be fast. Very fast. Jens Voigt would lead the way through Reeth in a daring, swashbuckling breakaway, only to be caught on the other side of Grinton Moor, but laying the foundations for a successful attempt on the hour record later that year.

However, in the summer of 2013, the driving was not fast, in fact, it was slow. Very slow. The A6108 was a winding road requiring caution, but the bigger issue was the scenery. There were just so many things needing their photographs taken – bridges like castles, moody market places and sheep against the skyline on rocky outcrops. Just the stuff that made the film in Welcome to Yorkshire's Tour bid such a dramatically compelling part of their audacious plan to host the race.

I started with Bedale Post Office. It was not on the race route, but I'd heard good reports of it and Bedale was clearly going to be a prime base camp for fans making a holiday around Le Tour. It proved impossible, with my cheap camera, to get the post office and church into a single photo, but Ian, the Sub-Postmaster, was enthused with the idea of welcoming all nations to Bedale as a gateway to the race. I stepped aside as each customer came in, their needs varying from parcels to pensions and from handbags to birthday cards. In between the friendly service, we exchanged phone numbers.

The morning was rapidly running away and I needed to get on the race route. I needed to drive north, but as I looked at my map I could see West Tanfield about six miles away in the opposite direction. I'd been there before, a few years earlier. It had been a bus trip of bell-ringers from the Barnsley & District Society. I remembered the splendid Marmion Tower, rich with French links from the 15th century, flanking the bell tower of the grand old church. There was a post office too according to Ketul's heat map. I had to go.

Thus came my first revelation of the day. Le Tour was eleven months away but here was a village that already had a committee organising weekly community events to build a fund to pay for a festival for the weekend of the race. Tour de Tanfield sunflowers emblazoned the lamp stands. The bell-ringers were involved and David and Susan running West Tanfield Village Stores and Post Office were in the engine room of the village website and social media strategy for the Tour de Tanfield.

They had seen my 'Sales and Cycling' article in the Subspace magazine for Sub-Postmasters the previous month. They had my number in their phone. It was like a blind date where the apple of your eye had already run a full credit reference on you before you turn up under the clock at noon.

'Rod. It's Rod. David it's Rod from that magazine.'

They even let me use their family toilet after a very welcome coffee from the recently refurbished convenience foods and cafe section of their store. Eleven months later they would go on to sell a year's worth of ice cream in a day. This was a village with a sense of purpose, in a world where not everyone had a sense of urgency. West Tanfield became a constant reference point and inspiration to me in the months to follow.

But Martin was waiting too. Quite some way north. Fifty-two minutes, in fact, according to the official Tour timetable at an average cycling speed of forty-two kilometres per hour. It would take rather longer in the car.

The road took me through Masham – predictably requiring a chat in the post office, another chat in the tourist information centre and a picture of the church spire. I would also be compelled to stop by the churches of East Witton and Middleham, and by a large pile of fresh gravel on Grinton Moor, a harbinger of grand tarmacking projects to come. Do you ever get a feeling like butterflies when you see new piles of gravel? Maybe you have to live near a Tour de France route …

I've cycled many roads in France and I know its yellow Michelin map series quite well, but I'd never been to Reeth. In fact, I'd never taken the Dales roads north of Leyburn, never been to Wensleydale and, embarrassingly, didn't even know of Buttertubs Pass.

Le Tour de France taught me so much about Yorkshire. I marvelled at a wealth of most idyllic towns, villages and moors that I had previously known nothing of. Mytholmroyd, Todmorden, Askrigg, Hawes, Reeth. All these places I came to know and love. Vive la France! Vive le Yorkshire! Bienvenue chez moi. Introduisez-moi chez moi.

Reeth was the icing on the cake of my post office visits that day. Descending from Grinton Moor, the splendour of Swaledale and Arkengarthdale opened out before me. Mysterious and richly historic-sounding places, like lands from Tolkien, but yet this was my home county. A new valley beckoned, a fabulous village green called out, a post office lured me in and shelf after shelf of Richmond Ales, Gladys's pies and scones, cycling mugs and rural keyrings pulled at my wallet. It was indeed with heavy bags that I left from Reeth Post Office. Not to mention a limited edition Tour-the-Dales T-shirt in a tin.

You too should pay a visit. They take a good parcel (I cannot in this book give postal advice). They do all sorts of banking activity (I cannot give financial advice). But they do good food and I will jolly well stick my neck out and recommend you get some. *Miam miam* as they say in France. Tuck in.

Martin would soon become a leader of the Tour Reeth Committee. A year later, tens of thousands of fans would line the roads from the village to the moor and the red polka dots on the white walls of his shop would call out to the media helicopters on high.

My day in the Dales took me to many other post offices, but they had no need of me. They would take active roles in their communities and Le Tour Yorkshire would be enriched by the part they would play. The same would be true for the farmers of the Dales, the markets, the brewers, the churches, the cheesemakers and the winemakers.

My trip had proven very fruitful in a sense of establishing business links and assessing readiness for the race. My journey had also reinforced my conviction that we had some beautiful churches bang on the race route. The next challenge would be to engage the bell-ringers.

The Yorkshire Association of Change Ringers handbook told me the practise nights and times for all the towers on the race route. Today was a Monday and so Aysgarth and West Tanfield were both scheduled to ring that evening. It would have been well nigh impossible for me to get the pair in on the same night as they both rang from 7.30 to 9 p.m. and were around an hour apart. I called them, but the phone rang out or the mobile reception was too weak. Oh to have had the National Farmers' Union Wi-Fi tractors around that day. They would come into their own for the fans next July.

I kept phoning. I was in Hawes, I was hungry and I got distracted again. I pulled up to look at my map and found myself outside Outhwaites Ropemakers. I'd pulled a good few of their ropes in my time so what a wonderful coincidence this was. They were very welcoming. In fairness they were slightly mystified by my enquiries a year in advance, but then it transpired they had stopped making bell ropes not long before my visit. A great shame. Nice toyshop though.

My stomach was rumbling but there was no time for a much needed bar meal. It was 6.30 p.m. and there was Askrigg church to be photographed yet and there were plenty more miles to go to get to Aysgarth. When, finally, I did arrive, there was no shop, a long queue in the hotel bar, and the tourist office at the Falls was shut.

There were also a number of distracting sheep in the area. The Dales had got their PR campaign running nice and early. #LostSheepYellowJerseys in particular had captured people's imagination. It involved 100 or so yellow stuffed sheep hidden throughout the Dales, with a prize draw if you spotted enough of them. Hands up this was another reason for me being late. In due course, real sheep would turn yellow too. And green. And polka dot red. But right now it was the stuffed sheep. I spotted one on Masham Town Hall. I spotted another on a wall nearby. Unwittingly I even captured the king of the pack (Jersey Jason) on the road to Wensley.

My camera was rammed with pictures of post offices and church towers and sheep. I was comfortable now finding hidden parking spaces, running down country lanes and taking shots of stuffed sheep as blokes in suits passed by in posh cars pretending they weren't doing the same. I tweeted to Adrian, The Dalesman editor. A left field story was shaping up, but he was finishing work for holiday that day, our car journeys were too far apart and the story slipped me by.

And then came the shock news that Aysgarth bell-ringers were on holiday too. It was as if the Dales was the home of the Aoutiens, that being a term for the residents of Paris who vacate the city en masse in August creating a virtual shutdown of many facilities.

This meant I was now without food, without bells and a long way from my fallback church of West Tanfield. The race was on. It would, of course, be a cautious, safe, respectful drive, flashing the tractors to pull out on their business and stopping unexpectedly when confronted by the grandeur of Wensley Church. This was one of the most magnificent churches I saw that day, simple and squat but almost castle-like. I was amazed that such a splendid church was actually congregationless, but I was equally reassured to know that it was safe in the care of The Churches Conservation Trust. There was a whole TV documentary I could construct about the 'living churches' and the cared for but no longer thriving places of worship along the Tour route.

That would be very interesting to film, but it was not going to solve my food issue. Nonetheless, a few minutes later, Campbells in Leyburn came up trumps with an interior like a TARDIS and the best crisps I've had in a long time. So, with a steering wheel covered in salt and vinegar, I finished my own breakaway down Stage One and parked up a short walk from West Tanfield church.

I parked outside The Bull Inn; a plan for later perhaps. Then I walked past that architectural gem of the Marmion Tower. The gateway to the bells was a little old door, like so many tower doors, nestling anonymously in a corner. Like the cupboard to Narnia, the first time visitor knows not what to expect, but is soon embraced by the closeness of the ancient stone walls and the timeworn spirals. These stairs, trodden by centuries of ringers' feet, led a short way up to another old door and then behold I was looking down into the warmth of the ringing chamber.

Christopher, the local Tower Captain, had happily received my voice-mail so it was not a total surprise when I appeared. I was welcomed by the band and we proceeded to make a joyful noise. We rang Plain Bob, we plain hunted and we did rounds and call changes. We were not ringing complex stuff but we were ringing with enthusiasm and enjoyment. Unburdened by the intensity, the advancement, the pressure of some bands, here we were having a laugh, ringing as friends, ringing with the spirit that Yorkshire churches would come to ring with all along the race route in a resonant welcome to the riders from across the world.

All of the band knew about Le Tour. Everyone was excited. No one was name dropping about who they were or what they did or what roles they were already playing for Le Tour. It was just good-hearted banter.

Eleven months later the heirs to the throne would walk through the Tour parties at West Tanfield. This was a well-connected community with a plan whose hugeness was so modestly understated but so professionally delivered. Like its post office in the morning, West Tanfield's ringers put this village firmly on my radar for Le Tour. A chat in the pub wrapped the day up nicely and the ringers were happy to try on my polka dot shirt and caps for the camera.

Le Tour de France in Yorkshire bonded communities and businesses and visitors in a wonderful way. I will go back to West Tanfield. I will go back. But it was not to be in the following year. There would be many more experiences like this giving me a bond with communities all over the county. Merci beaucoup, Le Tour. Merci beaucoup Welcome to Yorkshire. The grandest Grand Départ was built on foundations like these.

CHAPTER 10

IT'S ALL ABOUT THE BELLS –
AN APOLOGY TO DAVID WALSH

Professional cycling wound its way up and down some high peaks and dark valleys in 2013. Neither Alpe d'Huez with its twenty-one hairpins in a vertical kilometre, nor Cragg Vale, the longest continuous climb in England, could compete with the twists and turns and relentless revelations as Lance Armstrong's story moved into a new chapter, if not into a whole new library.

The sport of cycling must have felt like a punchbag. Or maybe an addict coming clean and fighting the hot and cold of rehab. It would, in many ways, be a tough year. As Alison in my team at work says, 'You have to take your medicine and you'll be better for it, whether you like it or not.'

Yorkshire skilfully surfed a PR blinder on the turbulent stories of the front pages, the back pages and the colour supplements. Bell-ringing was in demand too, which was partly why I got to offer an expected but very timely apology to David Walsh, face to face in *The Sunday Times* offices. David, of course, being the sports journalist of the year 2013 whose unrelenting doubt over Lance had led him through a decade and more of pain in fighting for truth and honesty and a new dawn from the omerta of the peloton.

Rewind fourteen years to the summer of 1999 … I was the editor of the Blue Line bell-ringing newsletter for the Central Branch of the Yorkshire Association of Change Ringers. Editor was rather a narrow title perhaps. The role was broad. You had to do the things that made the stories, ask people (without getting your hopes up) to write about them, then write it yourself, print it, copy it, staple it and post it. A real team effort.

The storyboard had actually been quite rich that year with tower open days, coach trips beyond the Yorkshire border and preparations for ringing in the new millennium. On the back of this confidence as a 'publisher', I had decided to complain to the sports editor of *The Sunday Times*.

'People love cycling,' I said, 'but you choose to ignore most races and when you do have something to say you just damn the riders.' 'This was really depressing for the reader,' I said.

David Walsh's boss of the day, Mr England, replied to me. Polite recognition and firm rebuttal. I was probably a bit naïve. I mean I'd never even tried a cigarette and goodness knows what wacky baccy was. The idea that sports stars were doped up wasn't really something I could relate to.

Perhaps I should have questioned though. Perhaps I should have looked at bell-ringing records of endurance feats too and, golly gosh, might they have had yeast supplements too? Certainly the heritage of bell-ringing included many towers in the eighteenth century being bricked off from the body of the church on moral grounds as ringers installed beer barrels in the belfry and led a life of bawdy behaviour high above the minimum wage farmhands tilling the fields below.

Lance would be stripped of his Tour victories, I would realise the narrowness of my viewing of the race, and Times Plus subscribers would be invited to an evening in Wapping to hear Shane Sutton of Team Sky talk cycling with David Walsh.

I fished out my carefully filed but scruffy draft letter to the newspaper. I found their nice letterhead reply too. I popped them into my laptop rucksack, held a day of meetings in London and Boris Biked over to Wapping for 7 p.m.

Shane would not be drawn on Wiggins v Froome. David was stoically respectful as he spoke of all the events in his recent career and in the mêlée afterwards I approached David with Mr England's reply to my letter. I only expected a quick word. I was surrounded by hardcore cyclists and commentators eager to share anecdotes. But David was intrigued by the correspondence. Perhaps in this world of auto archive, six-year document destruction timelines and clean desk campaigns, you don't find many original signed letters from the last century.

'Please could I take a copy?' David asked.

A copy? 'You can have the original', I replied. 'Let me just write my apology to you for doubting you. "David, you were right, I was wrong."'

I signed and dated it. It could and it should have been neater. But it was done and like the sport itself, I could move on too.

'By the way, I'm organising church bell-ringing for next year's Tour de France in Yorkshire. You'd be most welcome to pop in,' I said. I don't think that registered. But the warmth of the connection and the closure from giving an apology fourteen years overdue made the night.

Cycling owes a lot to David Walsh, newspaper editors owe a lot to David Walsh and we still need editors for bell-ringing newsletters. They're inviting a volunteer for a PR officer nationally for bell-ringing just as I write this.

I hope in some way that what we rang for Le Tour and how this book works out may somehow help the PR. Bell-ringing has been said to be the new cycling. By some people. Come on. Let's see.

CHAPTER 11

YELLOW PAGES –
WRITING THE GUIDE FOR THE TV COMMENTATORS

There is much majesty and mystery around Le Tour. The speculation and lobbying over the race route is perhaps only beaten by the two years of press hype that precede a US presidential election. Towns, villages, even whole countries make their bids to host a part of the race years in advance, but the final roads chosen remain a closely guarded secret until the special moment of fanfare at the announcement to the world's cameras.

When at last the race route does get unveiled, there is a global sigh of relief. Tens of thousands of camper van owners can be heard unfurling their maps as they are, finally, able to decide which Alp to park on for the summer.

Meanwhile, somewhere beyond the prying eyes of mere mortals, it is said that there is a mythical manuscript from which the media build their scripts – The Yellow Book. This is the guide that all the journalists and helicopter pilots refer to in planning their commentary and their flight paths. It is the source of rich anecdotes about chateaux and vineyards and other landmarks that the riders pass.

I have not seen this Yellow Book myself. I have not directly had confirmation from an Englishman who has yet. But, like the pursuit of the Holy Grail, I determined that if this book did exist, then it should be hunted down with vigour and its pages should be enriched with the imagery of the churches of the race route, whether they be cavernous cathedrals or pretty little parishes. The eyes of its readers should be excited by gritty church towers and their ears should ring with anticipation of the bells to be struck across the Dales.

Welcome to Yorkshire mentioned the Yellow Book at a roadshow and it became clear that there was a chance to submit content for editorial consideration. From early September I, therefore, began to phone and email as many churches and bell-ringers along the route as I could.

'Do you have a photo of your church that you could send me please, in order that the world's media may feast their eyes on the grandeur of your graveyard and on the splendour of your soaring spires? Do you have a three line description of your church, ideally with some historic links to France?'

'No,' they said. 'No. No. Noooooo!'

'Sorry', I thought to myself. 'Am I talking to evangelical, community-facing, story-telling parishes who want to welcome the world through their lychgate? Or are you hermits?'

Now don't get me wrong. Some did have photos. Some did have stories. But most didn't. Bizarrely, in a world of more smartphones than people, the idea that they might take a quick photo, seemed incomprehensible to them.

But let's reflect again on what I said a few chapters ago. Le Tour was still ten months away, many churches couldn't grasp the fact that a French sounding race was coming to their village and I was some unknown upstart trying to get people to take photos to attract helicopters with TV cameras. I guess it was a bit implausible … at the time … not now though.

Hang on, I thought. Perhaps The Church of England might have a PR officer that I could approach? A quick google soon led me to John Carter, communications officer for what was shortly to become the Diocese of West Yorkshire and the Dales. He and I linked up and, in a two-pronged assault, with new credibility, the stories flooded in to us. One of Yorkshire's own ringers, who had asked me to stop phoning him about the Tour, even came up trumps with a fine script.

Emboldened now with good material and some very strong French connections, the submission to The Yellow Book took shape. Four successive late nights (1 a.m., 2 a.m., 4 a.m., 3 a.m.) and it was done. Whether it made it to the final cut in Paris I may never know. Do you know? If you see Phil Liggett, Paul Sherwen, Carlton Kirby or any other of the world's TV commentators perhaps you could ask them. I truly would love to find out.

But whether it did or didn't make it, the exercise laid the foundations for an email contact list of churches around the route and John went from strength to strength with his own website Le Church Le Tour. The contents are now built into the website of the new diocese of West Yorkshire and the Dales.

Our submission to the Yellow Book was a cracker, if I do say so myself. We started with gravitas, thus:

> *Yorkshire is home to many beautiful churches. These splendid buildings will provide natural points of orientation and conversation for the riders as they enact their race plans and for the helicopters and media as they engage the global audience.*
>
> *With their tall towers, fine carvings and powerful Pennine gritstones these churches are an architectural and social embodiment of the themes with which Yorkshire 'welcomes the world' – true grit, Yorkshire 'en fete' and world class Yorkshire. With their bells they provide a richness to the soundtrack of the county.*

We then tantalised the world's media with the delights to be found in our churchyards. These were presented in the form of 'Ninety-nine Ideas for Churches to Get Involved in Le Tour'. You can read them in full yourself on John's website but they ranged from basic necessities to cutting edge post modern art.

At a practical level, churches could provide much needed watering holes, for the provision of a refreshing cuppa or the welcome release of the preceding one. Camping and car parks could also go down a storm. At a spiritual level there was much mileage to be had in cycling sermons and reflective spaces away from the madding crowds.

And on the artistic front what about roof banners, French music recitals and bikes suspended from church towers?

Now you're talking.

We concluded our submission with a 'Top Ten Towers' for Le Tour. I've now expanded that to cover all the race towers. You can read about them all in chapter 34.

CHAPTER 12

FROM PARIS TO PUDSEY

At the same time as composing the submission to the Yellow Book, a couple of other matters competed for my attention. Firstly, it was nearly November, the time for the BBC Children in Need appeal, for which Post Office was about to become the leading corporate partner. Secondly, and even more importantly, it was our tenth wedding anniversary and we had a romantic city break in mind for half term.

Two iconic locations quickly rose to the fore; Pudsey and Paris. Pudsey, nestled twixt the A6110 and A6177 loop roads of Leeds and Bradford, obviously had a strong link to Children in Need. It also had a Crown Post Office (within sight of a mighty fine church tower as it turned out). Its romantic allure was, however, on a different plane to Paris.

There was, therefore, little protest when I determined that our anniversary break should be in Paris and that my fundraising focus would be on Pudsey. A slight raising of eyebrows may have occurred when I unveiled my Children in Need Pudsey Ears headpiece in Paris and proceeded to take photographs of iconic Parisian architecture framed within the Pudsey spotted ears. No eyebrows were raised though at the very predictable presence of a Tour de France polka dot jersey in our holiday luggage. There had, after all, been ten months of Tour fever already in our house, starting back in December 2012.

It doesn't need me to tell you that Paris is a very beautiful city. Its museums, its churches and its boulevards are without parallel. So too its shops, its cafes and its open top bus tours. We did all of these things.

If you are planning to visit Paris with your loved one, I strongly recommend the bus tour at sunset, the cafes of Les Halles and a slow walk through the Louvre. If you are able to create a minor disturbance and a smokescreen, you can also tend to your Tour addictions by taking a photo of the Rue de Tivoli street sign, doing a 'compare and contrast' of Paris hire bikes versus London Boris bikes and wearing polka dots and Pudsey ears while fetching a late night bottle of Bailey's from the Champion mini supermarché. Champion, of course, being a former sponsor du Tour de France.

I only missed one BBC film crew planning session while in Paris. The #PudseyBikeRide was largely planned, manned and in hand by this point. With route and squad sorted and with The Yellow Book bid submitted, my mind was largely at rest and we had a fabulous anniversary break.

Sunset on the Seine from that open top bus and a slow drive round the fabulously illuminated Eiffel Tower were prime pieces of a perfect jigsaw in Paris. I confess that I would love to have seen that garden in Burley in Wharfedale where the Scouts and Guides built their own Eiffel Tower the next summer but, on balance, I reckon it'll be Paris again for city breaks. And anyway, part way through writing this, the Burley tower was sold on eBay. The buyer never turned up to collect it and so the Scouts used it for their 2014 bonfire. Hey ho.

Now, I admit that I do get diverted sometimes while writing this book. Please bear with me.

The last matter arising in Paris was the matter of bells. If you ask anyone in any country to name a bell-ringer, they will most likely say Quasimodo. I would like to confirm that his stereotype in no way matches the specification of the 21st century church bell-ringer. And if it did the names would be redacted.

Quasimodo, of course, rang the bells at Notre Dame, and the exciting news right now was that this was the year new bells had been cast and installed at Notre Dame. The queue for tower tours was impossibly long though, so this poor ringer didn't get anywhere near the bells, but there was a great display in the chancel of the cathedral.

Five months later, to celebrate the start of The Yorkshire Festival, the bell-ringers of St Marie's Roman Catholic Cathedral in Sheffield rang a quarter peal of congratulations to their friends in Notre Dame, to celebrate the first anniversary of those new bells in Paris.

Yorkshire Association Sheffield, South Yorkshire St Marie's Thursday 27 March 2014 1344 Plain Bob Major As part of Le Tour and the Yorkshire Festival. Celebrating one year since the installation of new bells in Notre Dame, Paris.	1 Janet I. Rogers 2 Emily V.R. Waters 3 Becky Holloway 4 Ben Newsam 5 Mike Sheeran 6 T.R. Palmer (C) 7 Christopher M. Bennett 8 Simon J. Reading

This was a wonderful moment for European harmony and for the *entente cordiale*. However, it occurred to me several times during this project that it would be great if we could go one step further and get church bells in France ringing at the same time as the bells of Yorkshire to launch the 2014 Tour. I made tentative enquiries about twinning towers ...

It's easy to add stuff to a 'to do' list though, but it's rather harder to get them done. That's one for next time, or for the film ... of the book ... of the bells ... of the bike ride.

Whatever, it would have to wait.

Pudsey, however, could not wait.

CHAPTER 13

NOVEMBER 2013 – THE PUDSEY BIKE RIDE

When I am at work, I have the privilege of heading up a great team of cake bakers in Chesterfield. It's actually a finance team, but that has never stood in the way of us rustling up table tops of tray bakes to raise money for Children in Need. When I say 'us' let me be clear and not steal the limelight, Carol leads the baking, I just take the photos. Well, not just the photos. I eat stuff as well. I'm not bad at that.

I've always worn a spotty shirt for it.

A few years ago, Children in Need had a great strap line of 'Show Your Spots and Let's Raise Lots'. I certainly had spots. They were great for Pudsey and, by happy coincidence, they hide the jam spills from doughnuts nicely.

The advent of Le Tour de France in Yorkshire suggested a whole new possibility. Cyclists in spots riding the race route, stopping for fundraising events and cake bakes at Post Offices along the way. I already knew several postmasters whose social media timelines were rich with gateaux. We could have groups of riders starting simultaneously at points all along the race route, riding tailored sections and then making a minor detour at the end. The detour being an added leg to all meet up at Pudsey Post Office.

I could see the graphics already, like the Norad Santa Tracker on the internet. We could have a grand countdown as all those riders and cakes converged on Pudsey.

I had the route, the stops, the riders, the story and the media on standby.

There was just one issue. 'It's all a bit too complicated to envisage,' said Alan, our head of corporate social responsibility. 'It's not a single simple journey, there are too many disparate segments and it doesn't give a compelling little image.' He was right. I was reluctant to hear it; I wanted it to work, but he was right.

So, back to the drawing board. The ride had to start or finish in Pudsey. This was essential. And amazingly, Pudsey Post Office had not actually been scripted into Children in Need for a few years since a school song in the previous decade.

My next challenge, therefore, was to find a Children in Need project for us to link in with. We googled, we checked with the BBC and the Boulevard Academy in Hull leapt out – a new school with a new vision for the city, supported by Children in Need and recently opened on the former site of Hull City Football Club.

Now Pudsey to Hull is a ride of around sixty-five miles. That is no small journey in itself, but you can't cycle the M62 and I wasn't desperately keen for us to ride through Leeds city centre at rush hour. So, what if we looped north? What if we visited Harrogate Road Post Office in Bradford, where Sam the postmistress has done so much for local charities?

I don't know if you have ever drawn a cycle path from Pudsey, out to north Bradford and then looped around the Harrogate area seeking the one and only crossing of the River Ouse at Cawood. But if you do, your route soon begins to look like bears' ears. Hmm. Pudsey Ears. #brilliant. Cracked it. Thank you Sam for diverting my pen on to that first ear.

Now, with the key points on the route established, the next challenge was to join the dots. Would there be enough roads, nice to cycle on, close to the ears?

I've subsequently found out that some sterling research and riding has been done by cyclists who use the Strava mapping tool. A year after our Pudsey Bike Ride, a chap from Salisbury rode a 187-mile route in a day which pretty perfectly drew a whole bicycle across East Dorset.

He didn't have the River Ouse to contend with. However, when you do eventually track down the only crossing for miles at Cawood, you'll find that Harrogate and Beverley give you nice northerly points for the tops of bears' ears and that Cawood and Market Weighton sit relatively comfortably on the head of the bear.

I signed up for several online mapping and drawing tools, oblivious to Strava. I became embroiled in more new passwords than is ever good for your blood pressure. And, as is my usual default, I sought comfort in three new Ordnance Survey maps of the tropics of Leeds, York and Hull plus a couple of maps of the Dales to complete my Tour de France set.

Ketul, in our London office, kindly ran me another heatmap of post offices within half a mile of the optimum ears route and we soon had a shortlist of seven branches where it seemed we could have a cracking fundraising party with the locals.

At this point I should again credit Alan, and Lorraine, with another very fair reality check.

'Come on Rod,' said Lorraine, 'do you seriously think that the team can ride 100 miles in the short daylight of November and make time for all those fundraising stops and photo shoots with the local mayors and nursery groups?'

Lorraine was right to question whether I had thought it through. Alan, although he didn't divulge all his reasoning, was hesitant too. He eventually explained why.

It turned out that a BBC film crew would be with us for the day. This would add a lot of excitement, but also a need for a Take One, Take Two, Take Three as we rode and re-rode into town. Alan also suspected that we'd all get distracted wanting photos with Warren Brown, star of *Luther* and *Hollyoaks*, who would be our celebrity for the day.

They were both right. I backed down. We dropped a couple of visits and Pudsey's left ear was subtly lowered from Harrogate to Wetherby, but still with a very nice rounded finish.

A year on, I treasure the email in which a very experienced senior press officer with Tour credentials confirmed that this was one of the most remarkable cycle routes he'd ever seen. Thanks Graham Poucher.

It was now eighty-five miles. It was shy of the previous headline grabbing 100, but Pudsey Ears across Yorkshire was winning hearts and minds. It was also getting in contention for the Paris catwalk, with some splendid multi-coloured spotty shirts to ride in, courtesy of One4All Gift Card UK, our close colleagues in supporting Children in Need at work.

We settled on five post office stops and a grand sprint finish into the Boulevard Academy. In the end, with a dark and rainy rush hour, the pack arrived in dribs and drabs, with Ash kindly going twenty-five miles out of his way (getting the 100 and more) to ensure everyone was accounted for. On television it was a smooth and orderly finish.

Time	Miles	Venue
09:00	0	Pudsey Post Office
09:30	8	Harrogate Road Post Office, Bradford
10:45	25	Wetherby Post Office
13:45	63	Market Weighton Post Office
15:45	83	Chanterlands Avenue Post Office, Hull
16:00	85	Boulevard Academy

Now, in addition to trying to do too many miles and stopping at too many events en route, I also wanted to make this a positive part of the company Cycle to Work campaign. I wanted it not just to be high intensity, weekend semi-pro riders who happened to work for the Post Office Monday to Friday. I wanted to generate some new recruits, new cyclists and new beneficiaries of the company Cycle to Work scheme.

You didn't need to be Sir Dave Brailsford, Team Sky and Team GB Cycling Manager, to realise that this could slow the peloton down. I, therefore, compiled an enthusiastic, inclusive, parallel ride where less 'semi-pro' riders could join for short bursts, get a lift ahead, then rejoin for the finish.

Obviously this soon became a logistical planning challenge.

Eventually, we settled on the core ride team who would do the whole thing – all eighty-five miles with quick photo stops. We then had the 'sprint section team' who would join for a few miles near Market Weighton and for the final leg into Hull.

I wanted to maximise the fun-time and fundraising time in each post office so I was in danger of shifting from player to player manager and ultimately to pure manager. This was getting complicated. And then there was the day job. And the Tour de France bell-ringing. And our tenth wedding anniversary.

And then Sally, who had been so patient and encouraging through this whole saga, reminded me of the spotty tape she had found in Paris. 'Wouldn't that look nice on your Pudsey Bike Ride?' she had said in a classy stationery shop near the Seine. Now, back in Yorkshire and on the cusp of filming day, I spent five hours cling-filming and taping to turn my shiny blue bike into a nice spotty bike. In fact, it is still spotty as I write this. Pudsey Spots, mind you. We also bought some polka dot tape in Paris but there was just never the time to swap the spots for Le Tour.

I'll get back to the ride soon ...

However, sometime early on in this project, Phil mentioned that he had a guitar (or five), Stacey mentioned that she could sing and Richard said that he'd written a few lyrics before. Well that's a potent combination isn't it? A couple of lunchtimes in the 'creativity room' and we had a single 'Riding Out For Pudsey Bear'. It sold 200 copies. In fact, it sold out. All for Children in Need. But the world premiere live acoustic gig in the card and Sellotape aisle at Market Weighton Post Office was the icing on the bike.

Now, we had a great time completing our ride. I reckon I might write a separate book about that, as I do need to get back to the story of bells, but suffice to say that cake bakes across Yorkshire, send offs from Pudsey Bear, riding with a BBC camera strapped to my saddle post and being welcomed into the children's project in Hull were just absolutely wonderful moments of a great day.

You'd also be welcome to ride the route yourself. It starts from outside Pudsey Post Office, which is just down the road from the bells of Pudsey church, wherein may lie another idea for another day ...

CHAPTER 14

THE YORKSHIRE FESTIVAL – TO BID OR NOT TO BID

Soon after the announcement that Le Tour was coming to our county, Welcome to Yorkshire issued a couple of invitations. Firstly, they encouraged fans to come forward to form a 10,000 strong organisation of Tour Makers to act as welcomers and as roadside marshalls. Secondly, they announced the Yorkshire Festival of Arts and Culture, for which people were invited to submit bids to deliver headline events and a fringe programme.

To bid or not to bid, that was the question. Were it nobler to stand roadside cheering the riders, or nobler to be a Tour Maker? Or were it nobler to bid to host an event for the Yorkshire Festival as a warm-up gig for Le Tour?

If you have never watched the Tour roadside, especially in France (as I would once have said) or especially in Yorkshire (as I would now say) then I forgive you if this question does not set your pulse racing. I forgive you for not being excited about the prospect of standing in a half square metre patch (aye, a half square metre if you're lucky), for six hours, with no mobile reception, with fading camera batteries, with bags of croissant and with a modesty bottle should you need to relieve yourself and can't get to the impossibly small number of public conveniences in a community where the biggest event to hit town is usually the carol singers at Christmas. I forgive you for being oblivious to what is possibly the greatest sense of community togetherness that you will experience outside of Royal Weddings, Jubilees and Regent Street on the day Barnsley FC got promoted to the Premier League.

Let there be no doubt – to be a roadside fan is wonderfully rewarding. It can also be an endurance feat.

Roadside fans I applaud you. Brothers in arms. Brothers in farms. Brothers and sisters on drystone walls the length of the Grand Départ. Hurrah!

I wanted to be roadside and, sure enough, that would be possible. But, I wanted to be a Tour Maker too. And that one got away – it clashed (a) with togetherness as a family on race weekend and (b) with bell-ringing.

So my decision was made, the bid would be for a Festival event. But would it be for a 'grand commission', a large scale, high quality project with national significance or would it be for a lower key D.I.Y. event not attracting any funding and simply benefitting from a bit of PR?

Church bell-ringing, with its dominant venues along the route, its vantage points looking on to the race, and its opportunity to partner with arts and community events in the body of the church or churchyard surely presented a credible foundation for a big ticket idea for the Festival. There were obvious opportunities in music and song, fabulous auditoriums for theatre and acres of space for lots of small art or one or two pieces of big art. You know, like the Tate Modern. In fact, you know what, I think this is worth looking at again in 2016 and 2018 …

However, in the autumn of 2013, looking ahead to the Festival, and bearing in mind that I already had a more than full-time job leading a finance service centre, I needed to ensure that I didn't bite off more than I could chew.

I needed to hone my ideas and I needed to understand what other people were doing. We might be able to inspire each other. I had some contacts from the Tour roadshows and people had been interested in bells, but in fairness those people were landowners, local business leaders, celebrities, band leaders, theatre producers and the like. They did not need bells to make their events fly.

I increasingly felt like the Monty Python accountant thinking about becoming a lion tamer.

However, I had Twitter.

As it happened, the decision would be taken out of my hands. But I get ahead of myself.

As I was saying, I had Twitter …

CHAPTER 15

EVENT LEADERS – SUMMIT AT CRAGG VALE

Living, as I did, in social media, I had my finger on the pulse of leftfield events in Yorkshire and of armchair commentators who now and again would spawn the most wonderfully ridiculous and compelling ideas. With a year to go, I was beginning to see a disparate bunch of local folk with global ideas popping up all over the race route. Among these were the good folk of Cragg Vale whose ambition was to break the world record for the longest line of bunting.

It was during the Mediterranean stages of Le Tour 2013 that I first became aware of Cragg Vale, the longest continuous incline in England. Cragg Vale Corner made it into the ITV Cycling coverage. I've lost my 2013 recordings now, but I'm pretty sure that Ned Boulting talked to them in Nice or somewhere comme ça.

This was Yorkshire in France. And the thing was I knew a bit about Nice, about the great cycling to be had in the mountains around the city and the excitement of Paris-Nice 'The Race to the Sun' early in the annual cycling calendar. I hadn't, however, heard of Cragg Vale, four miles north of M62 junction twenty-two as the crow flies.

Looking back, I am more than a little embarrassed to say that. Embarrassed as a cyclist not to know of Cragg Vale's historic climb. Embarrassed as a Yorkshireman to not know of its grandeur. And embarrassed as a bell-ringer given the magnificent eight-bell tower of Mytholmroyd standing proudly over the sharp turn across the River Calder as you ride in from Hebden Bridge and turn south to start the long slope to the summit.

I've said it before but I learnt a huge amount about my home county as a result of Le Tour de France coming to Yorkshire.

I registered the name Cragg Vale on my 'people to call list'.

Weeks later, I investigated Cragg's contours on a 1:50,000 Ordnance Survey map. I admired the consistency of the relentless ascent and agonised over how to fit a visit in without getting stuck in the usual traffic jam past IKEA. What struck me more powerfully than the iconic climb though was the bunting project, the idea that Cragg Vale would challenge the Guinness World Record for the longest line of bunting, held at the time by BBC Hereford and Worcester at 32,808ft and four inches. That, in turn, was under threat, apparently, from an ambitious group of Australian barbecue fans. In time, of course, our Yorkshire heroes would succeed with a 12,115m continuous length of bunting, encompassing 59,939 flags stretching from Mytholmroyd to an abrupt, and deliberate, finish just past the summit of Cragg Vale and, as reported in *The Daily Telegraph*, just short of the Lancashire border. This was an audacious project. This was the spirit of Le Tour. This needed linking in with. I followed their account on Twitter and I began to gather press cuttings about bunting.

I also, by happy coincidence, was able to volunteer to serve in Halifax Post Office when they found themselves temporarily short of staff in August 2013. Halifax, it turned out, was six miles from Cragg Vale. With roadworks it would seem much further.

I don't have satnav, but I do have a rich stash of OS maps. Nevertheless, amid the deep dales, tall towers and woolly one ways of Halifax I was soon lost.

It was a wet day. A very wet day.

I once did a cycle tour in Norway and encountered a couple of wet days there. As part of my training for Norway, I read *Peer Gynt* and I immersed myself in the imagery of pine trees and trolls. I was not expecting this to be trumped on the Cragg, but it was.

If you followed the 2013 Tour on Twitter, you may recall someone tweeting a magnificent picture of 'Hedge Monster'. I now came face to face with this beast in the August downpour. A similar storm in the next valley led to one of those eight-foot holes in the road, into which a parked car had plunged. Cragg's B6138, thankfully, did not cave in but Hedge Monster would not have been out of place looming from such a hole. As it was, he appeared ominously between my overworked windscreen wipers. His baleful eyes penetrating deep into my car and his silence asking where my bicycle was. How dare I *drive* up this hallowed road?

Though the rain was hard and the road was narrow, I found a place to pull in and through the flap flap of the windscreen wipers I took aim. There would be monster 'denialists', you know, like those people who say those Scottish photos show branches from trees not the curving spine of Nessie, but I would have the best evidence I could. If this was to be my end, my Twitter timeline would tell my story, and future navigators would be forewarned to avoid coming to the same sticky end as me.

Click.

It would be good to see this work of art on a sunny day, but it was fitting to have seen it in the rain, this beast of the road, looming from the mist like a tribute to Stephen Roche as he emerged from the fog of La Plagne, silhouetted by car headlights, surging to the Maillot Jaune in the 1987 Tour de France. I was able, thankfully, to continue without the oxygen mask that Roche needed. Hedge Monster, I salute you.

A few minutes later, slightly bedraggled, I met Vernon. I had driven a little further up the road to The Robin Hood pub, I had paddled through turbulent puddles and I was now standing transfixed in a tavern soon to become the French Embassy to Calderdale. I was captivated by the sight of prototype bunting, I was heartened by a half pint and I was in awe of the enormous Yorkshire Grand Départ map on the wall, not to mention the top notch collection of cycling photos.

Six months later, Bernard Hinault, five times winner of Le Tour de France, would stand there. Indeed he would cycle there, he would sit there and he would have a pint, a whole pint, not just a half. That's real cycling for you. He'd even use a photograph taken on my phone for his Twitter account header. But that's another chapter.

Anyway, 'Great photos. Love this leaderboard,' I said, looking at the chalked-up list of times in the doorway to The Robin Hood. 'Are you a cyclist?'

We talked bikes. We talked beer. We didn't talk bells, I don't think. I'm not sure that we talked bunting either that day. Vernon sold me a Cragg Vale Community Association calendar for 2014 and introduced me to the landlord still mopping water out from behind the bar after the day's downpour. Warm-hearted folk. Nice beer. Nice crisps. Exceptional Tour de France wall.

Many hours later, back in Sheffield, my phone buzzed with the increasingly frequent announcement of a message for me on Twitter.

'I think you met my husband, Vernon, tonight, in The Robin Hood,' tweeted the cycling fan behind the Cragg Vale 2014 social media account. Let's, for simplicity, call her Sharon. Oh my word. Oh my goodness. Not only had I been chatting to a real gent, I'd connected with the dynamic forces behind the bunting project. Such ambition, but such modesty.

A network began to form and soon we were linked in with a hugely enthusiastic group of cycling tweeters from Ripon to Elland to Holmfirth.

'We should meet,' we tweeted. We agreed that we should compare notes and see how we could play a small part in helping deliver the grandest Grand Départ ever. After much checking of diaries we settled on Tuesday 24 September 2013. 7 p.m. to be precise at The Robin Hood; sorted.

Now it's awful to be late. That feeling of pressure, of self inflicted failure, fear of missing the meeting, fear of missing the chips. Truly awful. Thankfully though the M1 was fine that September evening. The M62 was fine. Even the IKEA junction was clear. It was the roads around Halifax that got me. Again.

The towers played their part in delaying me too. I mean, who wouldn't stop when they saw Wainhouse Tower looming over them? Past the terraces, past the flats, there was the biggest boldest stone tower I had ever seen (excluding Emley Moor TV transmitter which, of course, is reinforced concrete anyway). And behind it were cobbled streets, beautiful cobbles like the Spring Classics ride on in northern France and Belgium, but with the twist of being on 1 in 5 slopes,

I had to stop and take a photo. This was Wainhouse Tower, 275 feet high and originally intended as a chimney for John Wainhouse's dye works, following the Smoke Abatement Act of 1870. It ended, however, unused by the dye works but as a controversial viewing platform in a dispute about privacy with neighbouring landowner Sir Henry Edwards. It is the tallest structure in Calderdale and the tallest folly in the world.

The meeting was starting in five minutes and then came the roadworks.

Now, with my Tour hat on, I was thrilled by the roadworks. Oh yes. This was fresh tar, fresh racing surfaces, fresh standing ground for the fans. This would be a delight for the race. It was just that it was being laid on what was the only bridge I had seen over the Calder in Mytholmroyd. I had no idea how else to get over the river to Cragg Vale.

The traffic lights were green, the steam of the tar dispersed, there weren't actually any cones formally blocking the road and the asphalter was far away between the high mill cottages. Perhaps this bridge was okay after all. Perhaps the road closure was a bit further up the Cragg. So I turned left. I had so far just been on an A road, the A646. Now I was on Stage Two of Le Tour. And then it confronted me … the vast line of orange lights, the renewed clouds of steam … the absence of cars …

This was not the merchandising caravan that precedes Le Tour. Oh heck, I'd only managed to get myself on the inside of the roadworks, marooned between Tour de France tarmackers, fresh asphalt on one side, freshly scraped road on the other.

The meeting had started and to cap it all it was pretty poor mobile reception. Somehow, praise be, I got a text through to the pub. They were rapidly moving down the agenda. The butties were going fast, the drumsticks proving a winner and the thick cut chips almost extinct.

By goodness knows what fortune, I drove back out of the roadworks the way I came and as far as I know the peloton never got stuck in any tyre ruts on Cragg Road. Vic texted me directions to a second bridge and a secret tunnel near the doctor's surgery and in half a mile or so I was back on Cragg Vale beyond the orange lights of the asphalt spreaders.

When I finally arrived at The Robin Hood, we were in the upper room. This was the hallowed carpet where Bernard Hinault would imbibe his ale. In the event that you get to visit this mecca of cycling, please note the following directions. It is easy to get distracted and lost.

You go in through the front door. Focus your eyes ahead of you as you climb the step. It is tempting to look longingly up the road, the tarmac the Tour raced up. If you don't look ahead you will trip on the step and look very, very silly on the floor.

You then pass the Cragg Leaderboard on your right. Pay respect to this.

After a false flat section of around six feet, probably to help 'run off' from the next rain, you will be surrounded by fellow Tour enthusiasts at the bar. Beware. Echelons can form here. The cunning rider can manoeuvre quickly to the bar, but is likely be disqualified by the very fair judge at the bar. Accept the echelons. They are also known as queues.

Finally, breakaway to the left, up a short sharp ascent to the rarified atmosphere of the Tour room. In my case, the 'committee' were bunched in a tight pack around the remaining chip bowls on the table on the left. However, like Robert Millar at Guzet-Neige in the 1988 Tour, it would be easy to take a false right here, lured by the bunting and snatch defeat from the jaws of victory, capturing a selfie by the Tour wall but missing the last chip butty.

When I referred to an agenda earlier, in fairness, it was more of a guest list. Basically, the plan was to migrate from tweeting to meeting with lots of eating. And to determine how we might encourage and help each other.

The first thing I learnt, in the build up to the meeting, was what a macaron is. Now this may seem like an irrelevant diversion to you, but hold on. You cycle, therefore you likely eat cakes? You ring bells, therefore you likely eat cakes? Now, I happened to go on a rant on Twitter during the *Great British Bake Off*, to ask ' ... what exactly is a macaron for goodness sake?' Macaroons are coconut bakes. But macaron surely is a typo. And behold, from nowhere, Medici Macarons replied to confirm the huge difference between a macaron and a macaroon. A macaron being a French sweet meringue-based confection made with egg white, icing sugar, granulated sugar, almond powder or ground almond and food colouring.

Now I don't know how many planetary alignments you have encountered, but here was one. Medici Macarons lives near Cragg Vale and oh my word do you know who supplied the desserts for our meeting. Medici Macarons. And she had chosen to test a prototype polka dot macaron on us.

It was a winner for me. Potentially the world's first Tour de France themed polka dot macaron and I was there.

But we did more than eat. We did actually discuss serious plans for Le Tour. Individually, members of the group all went on to great things in the Grand Départ. I'm still not sure I know everyone's actual names, I'm dreadful at remembering names if I'm honest, and some of them have closed or changed their Twitter accounts since Le Tour. So let me refer to them by Twitter name or website address where I can. Do look them up.

Here's what they went on to do:

Le Tour Ripon	Mass participation rides and renowned cyclist speaker events
Dales Active	Various events and raising the profile of businesses in The Dales
Le Tour Ripponden	Organising rides and producing awesome bike themed clothing
Le Tour Elland	Mass accommodation and rides for Tour fans
Le Tour Holmfirth	Mass participation rides, schools involvement and town steering group
Cragg Vale 2014	Hush hush hosting of Bernard Hinault visit. And world record bunting
Bells and Bikes	The stuff that encouraged you to buy this book in the first place

We had a fine time sharing ideas. Most of us were actually in the room, but Rob of Le Tour Ripon skyped in. He walked from room to room on a buffering video link, hoisting his red wine glass in faux Frenchness to disguise his angst at missing the chips.

Our final guest, the activist known as Le Tour Holmfirth, was caught up with school meetings, but submitted an excellent paper for noting. He had a very fine mock-up logo and my word what great things he went on to do with bikes and schools in Holmfirth. And indeed continues to do. Check him out on social media: a new cycling club, a recycled bikes charity, public art projects, sneaking Holmfirth stickers on to the Team Sky car and turning the Holme Valley dotty. Fabulous stuff.

Our meeting also discussed a grand plan for hosted artworks all along the roads of Cragg Vale and Ripponden Bank. It would be artwork linking the valleys. I don't know how that actually turned out. Maybe that was one dream too far. Next time perhaps?

As for bells, people liked the idea. I shared the paper that I mentioned back in chapter 7 and bizarrely this seemed to be cutting edge planning. The fact that I had no ringers on board yet seemed irrelevant to the meeting. The idea was good and the race was months away. The verdict was that it would work. This group became a source of much inspiration in the months to come.

Sharon even sat in the back of the lead Tour car, the day Bernard Hinault had his bike ride and pint on the Cragg. There are many more stories to be told, but it would be rude of me to take those from the owners.

Informed, inspired and refreshed we drove off into the darkness. I got lost in Tour roadworks on Ainley Top under the M62, but my spirits remained high with the perfume of the tarmac. A good night was had by all. I was home by 1.30 a.m. and in bed by three and on the train to London by eight.

I started the last chapter with the question, 'to bid or not to bid?' Was it going to be worthwhile submitting a formal festival event bid to Welcome to Yorkshire or would it be simpler and less vain just to get on with organising bells?

The decision, in the end, was not really mine …

CHAPTER 16

DECEMBER 2013 – BELL-TING NEWS – 'YES, WE WOULD LIKE BELLS FOR LE TOUR'

'Just following up on our conversation about church bells pealing around the TdF route. Wondered if we could set up a meeting to discuss further.'

Thus ended Dee's email, head of communications at Welcome to Yorkshire.

Now, how would one reply to that? Does Geoff Boycott like batting? Do Yorkshire Puddings like gravy? Er, yes I'd be delighted to meet.

Looking back, the whole thing is like some strange dream. Did it happen? Didn't it happen? Did I simply hallucinate after too many late nights trawling OS maps, emailing unresponsive ringers and plotting cycle rides like bear's ears?

On balance, I think it did happen. Twelve inches of plans and articles and press releases on my bookshelf suggest something took place. Eleven gigabytes of photos leave a heavy fingerprint on our laptop. And you can just see the edge of my shoulder in polka dots in Bernard Hinault's Twitter profile photo. Sorry, did I mention that before.

So yes, it must be true.

And Dee's email in December 2013 was one of those pivotal moments in the story.

It was always a bit chicken and egg. I was always out on a limb, making proposals but not knowing if the ringers would actually come along to make it possible. I was fighting a tide of sentiment through the whole thing that said ' … the roads are closed and we don't think we can walk there … ' (despite being keen hikers and regularly posting photos of moorland on Facebook).

I had to convince the ringers it was possible. I had to convince Welcome to Yorkshire it was possible. The latter was proving easy. The ringers were a bit harder to rope in.

In fairness it was still seven months away. But I'd been on the case for a year already. I was on tenterhooks about how many bells would ring in July.

Most other people were still deciding what to buy for Christmas. There was always something else more pressing. Mind you, bells are pretty important at Christmas. In fact, if there was one thing I learnt and deployed when kick-starting it all over again for the 2015 Tour de Yorkshire, it was not to hassle bell-ringers with summer cycling ideas in December. I waited until January the next time. Well, err, 1 January shortly after lunch. Hmm.

What I needed, back in December 2013, was commitment and evidence, from the top, before I could confidently go much further in communicating with ringers and in making offers for Le Tour.

This time, the authenticity of the request from Welcome to Yorkshire gave it gravitas.

So far it had just been me, a recently infrequent ringer, trying to engage an Association of Change Ringers whose members had in many cases forgotten who on earth I was, trying to get them excited about a global sports event which they still didn't seem to know was happening. And, if it was happening, it was months away. Dee's note, however, brought some realism to it.

After months of solo groundwork, I soon had the incoming Association President and myself in the diary to meet at Welcome to Yorkshire's offices on Tuesday 17 December.

Yorkshire being a vast county, Andrew and I lived hours apart. Our contact had been sporadic and whilst I had pre-circulated an agenda, neither of us knew exactly what the other would put on the table for Welcome to Yorkshire. It was, therefore, with some excitement that I first clapped eyes on the artwork that he unveiled at the meeting.

Andrew had recognised the importance of a catchy image and he'd knocked up a fusion of bikes and bells.

While cricketers celebrate the number 100, distance runners hold 10,000 in awe and darts players aim for 180, bell-ringers live for factorial numbers. These factorials represent the number of different, unrepeated, changes that can be rung on a defined number of bells. That is to say, the number of different sequences that can be struck, where every bell rings once in each sequence and then adjacent pairs in the sequence swap and ring again, with no repetition occurring in the order.

Seven factorial (7x6x5x4x3x2x1) is 5,040 and this is the milestone defined as a 'peal'. Whether you have five bells, six bells, ten bells or more in your tower, 5,040 is universally recognised as the benchmark number of changes in a peal.

You could, of course, ask why seven factorial set the gold standard for peals; why not six factorial or eight factorial? In practical terms, 5,040 changes, taking around three hours to ring is more of a challenge than six factorial (720 changes) which takes only around half an hour and eight factorial (40,320 changes) which would take a whole day. Moreover, in composition terms many tears had been shed in the late 17th and early 18th centuries by ringers trying to compose a 'true' (unrepeating) peal on seven bells.

The widely accepted and highly acclaimed first such peal was eventually achieved at St Peter Mancroft, Norwich in 1715. Its tercentenary attracted much global celebration on 2 May 2015, 300 years to the day since that first peal. This, coincidentally, was the same day that Stage Two of the 2015 inaugural Tour de Yorkshire passed several churches whose bells were being rung by members of the Beverley and District Society of Change Ringers as a glorious welcome to the race.

Andrew created a bicycle logo around the number 5,040. The zeroes were the wheels, the five gave it handlebars and the four spread itself out a bit to create the frame.

Andrew made a fair point at the county AGM a few months later when he said 'Rod may do more cycling, but I do more ringing,' however, he deployed sensitivity to both with perfection at our December meeting.

I can see that you are perhaps not as excited as I was by this or as proud as Andrew was. It never made it on to ITV Cycling in 2014, but its time will come again. It is one of those quiet gems from ringing for Le Tour.

There were three things to watch on arrival at Welcome to Yorkshire's offices in December 2013. Firstly, there was a wheel Christmas tree, and no that's not a typo. It was a wheel tree. It stood proud in the courtyard, yearning for nightfall to show its colours to the best.

Then, in reception we were greeted by a Woolly Bike – the prototype, the genesis, the godfather of Woolly Bikes. Like my Cragg Vale experience, I had been oblivious to Woolly Bikes until this moment and I would not come to meet its maker for a few months yet. But this bike, this every-day bike, dressed in the finest knitwear made a statement of intent. This was Le Tour, but not as we knew it. Woolly Bikes would become one of my favourite events of the Yorkshire Festival, the warm up for Le Tour. Pleased to meet you. Bienvenue à Yarnstorming.

The third thing was the Tour de France themed armchair. Ronnie Corbett never sat in a chair like this and DFS have never had a double discount on a seat like this. Le Tour. Le Chair. Sans rider. That was hard core, Tour furniture. I wish I'd sat in it. I wish I'd heard of selfies back then. But I hadn't.

Finally, there was Tower Works. There were not three but four things to watch for on arrival at Welcome to Yorkshire's offices. Imagine a church tower, plopped on to a factory and sited bang opposite the offices of the organisation which had so delighted Paris that Le Tour was coming to Yorkshire. Yes, their offices sat under the watch of Tower Works. Destiny.

So there we were. Andrew, me, Dee and Mark, manager of the Yorkshire Festival. Dee and Mark wanted to know about churches on the race route and the synchronisation of ringing as a welcome to the caravan, the mo-torcade of advertising vehicles that precede the riders.

Ringers had already said that they wanted to see the riders and Dee confirmed that they didn't want bells drowning out the commentary on the riders. So it was agreed that we would focus on ringing for the caravan.

We explained whether the churches were roadside or up side streets, we mentioned scope for TV cameras to visit towers and we hoped vicars were aware of Le Tour as they took wedding bookings for the weekend of 5 July. It could be the biggest ever crowd in a wedding photo or the road closures might wrongly create a suspicion that there was indeed some rea-son why the couple may not lawfully be married. Thankfully greater minds than us were ensuring continuity of transport systems. And I have to say from my own experience, and from Derek and Ronalda's experience (whom I will introduce to you soon), that the trains and buses did a crack-ing job in the eye of the storm.

What was equally exciting as the request for bells on race day though was Welcome to Yorkshire's interest in PR for bells generally and their desire to help with the pressing need for new recruits to keep bell-ringing alive and well for the future.

This was a theme through the whole of Yorkshire's Grand Départ – it wasn't just about the bike. It was about the community, the heritage, the bringing together of different worlds.

Rarely can there have been a greater opportunity to get church bell-ringing centre stage in world sporting affairs. Thank you Welcome to Yorkshire.

CHAPTER 17

JANUARY 2014 – THE YORKSHIRE FESTIVAL.
THE LAUNCH, THE CLASH AND THE WOMBEL

Christmas came and went.

The shopping was done. The ringing was done. Big Ben struck twelve, and the crowds roared as we entered the year of the 101st edition of Le Tour de France. The year promised by Gary Verity to yield the grandest Grand Départ ever. The year of Le Tour Yorkshire.

We could stop prefacing year with 'next'. We were now in the present tense. And yes, I was still tense about whether enough ringers would actually get on board with the project.

'Happy New Year, Gary' we all tweeted. What a hero. How he had changed our lives. How must he be feeling now?

If I'm tense about bell-ringing, how must he be feeling hosting the most northerly Grand Départ ever? And doing so in a county where people love nothing better than a good moan about skips, bins and potholes (of which our roads had plenty).

But Gary had a strong conviction about Le Tour. He won over the team at Welcome to Yorkshire to the madness of his idea. He won over the county. Indeed he won over the country, underlined by the prime minister hosting a cabinet meeting in Welcome to Yorkshire's offices.

I would urge you (and I am not on a commission for referrals) to read the inside story of Yorkshire's bid in *Two Days in Yorkshire* by Peter Cossins and Andrew Denton. There are wonderful and emotional surprises throughout. Christian Prudhomme (Tour director) and Bernard Hinault (five times Tour winner) became virtual Yorkshiremen and three million roadside fans became honorary citizens of France. Their citizenship being partly due to the absolute love of France that our towns and villages exuded and partly due to some sort of European bylaw by which the roads the Tour races on temporarily become part of France as the race passes by. Or so I read somewhere.

Sir Dave Brailsford, Team Sky and Team GB coach, summed it up nicely when interviewed after Stage One: 'Endless crowds. You expected them to stop round the corner but there was no end.'

Anyway, as I said, 2014 was here at last. It was now time to step up a gear.

It was time for a new set of communications to churches on the race route. This would become a sizeable job as (a) I'm a bit of a perfectionist, (b) no one else was helping, and (c) it was an excuse to indulge my addiction to post offices and to trying out bulky envelopes in those special Perspex measuring things on the counter.

The post would eventually be despatched in February half-term holiday, with Mrs Bellsandbikes kindly saying 'do you need an hour to finish those letters?' Sixteen hours later I was indeed ready.

However, back to the bells.

It was Wednesday 22 January when I got the phone calls from Natalie and Jenny at Welcome to Yorkshire. 'We're hosting a media launch for the Yorkshire Festival Programme, in the Trinity Centre, Leeds next Wednesday. This has to remain confidential, but would you be able to get some bells there?'

I don't know exactly how familiar you are with campanology, but church bells individually tend to weigh half a ton or more (hundreds of kilogrammes if you are reading this in French) and they are firmly fixed in sturdy wooden or steel frames a long way up large stone towers that don't typically move very easily. Or indeed at all.

This was certainly an opportunity that I wanted to help with, but I had a number of hurdles to overcome.

Fundamentally I needed to determine whether bells were indeed possible in a shopping centre and then, as the flipside of the same question, I needed to find out if anyone could come and ring them.

At the next level there were then some options around the bells:

1. Church bells
2. Handbells
3. A mobile belfry
4. Some thing I wasn't yet aware of, but was hoping would come to my rescue.

Church bells, for the reasons already stated, were unlikely to be a goer.

Nor was a mobile belfry. Such things do exist but I just didn't know anyone who had access to one.

I, therefore, focused my energy on handbells. On the positive side these were easily portable and lovely to listen to. On the downside I didn't have any, and I wasn't sure I knew anyone else who did.

So, again, I phoned a friend and thankfully it became clear that there were lots of church bell-ringers who were handbell ringers and they were interested in helping.

This was good news. Very good news. Especially as the launch was only seven days away.

But one step forward, one step back. It wouldn't be simple. And my first blow was self-inflicted.

In the heat of the moment, shaping my plans at 11pm, it was easy to forget that other people have lives to lead, jobs to do and sleep to have. And indeed that I too had a job which required me taking at least a few hours' sleep in between sessions at the desk.

The fact of the matter was that I was not a full time event organiser. Or part time. Or job share. In fact, I was an accountant with a demanding day job to deliver. An accountant involved in reshaping our finance team vision and co-hosting a national team event on 29 January, the same day as the Festival launch.

The Festival event in Leeds was from 9.30 a.m. to 11.30 a.m. Even Bradley Wiggins could not have made it from there to Nottingham for the start of our finance event. You'd have to be more than a gold medal time triallist to do that. You'd need to be Doctor Who.

I was neither.

And so, with much gnashing of teeth, I internalised my issues and accepted that the Festival launch was one event I was going to have to miss. The blow was softened by the happy coincidence of us having a guest speaker from Sky's Finance Team with us in Nottingham. So while I missed out on the bikes and the Yorkshire stuff, I did at least get to meet a real life member of Team Sky. Well, an accountant from Sky's finance team anyway.

My second and third blows were not unrelated.

The handbell ringers who had been so keen to help also had day jobs to do. With hospitals to work in, lecture theatres to present in and schools to teach in, another tranche of ringers slipped away.

Thankfully there was a second wave of possible ringers in the student population and the retired. But goodness me, the early morning must have put the students off and one's passion for Leeds rush hour seems to wane somewhat with retirement.

And then there were none.

So here was my issue. The Yorkshire Festival programme was about to be unveiled to the world's media and bell-ringing was a headline act. We had over 300 bell towers across the county and potentially thousands of ringers, but we couldn't get anyone to Leeds for a free buffet and a slot on the local news.

So what about pure handbell ringers? If the church bell-ringers couldn't make it what about a handbell orchestra?

Google introduced me to a handbell band in Sheffield. Through them I reached out to county leaders. But by now it was truly too late in the day. It was just not possible to get an orchestra together at such notice. I guess that's kind of obvious though. Perhaps, if it had been possible, I would have already become a full time event organiser rather than an accountant.

As it was, I remained an accountant. An accountant who was feeling a bit low.

In the Grand Tours of pro-cycling, there is a point in the mountain stages when the big men are at their lowest – exhausted after 120 miles of headwind, in the shade of the valley floor, confronted by a seemingly endless wall of hairpin bends reaching to the clouds. It is there that the little climber in the peloton can punch back with a birdlike ascent to success.

I am not that cyclist.

In fairness, I do wear polka dots and I have 'raced' up Alpe d'Huez. I only saw two other cyclists on the climb and I held them off. I was beaten only by the ski resort dustbin lorry. Nevertheless, I am not that birdlike climber.

However, I do know Derek and Ronalda Johnstone – the ringing world's equivalent of the 'super domestiques' of Team Sky. We had stared into the jaws of defeat on Stage One of Le Tour Bell-ringing. Now, however, we had two fresh pair of legs (and more importantly arms) to get back in the ringing race. Move over peloton. Here comes the belloton.

'We can take the Wombel to Leeds,' they said.

'The what?'

'The Wombel. It's just that it's a bit heavy … '

The Wombel, it transpired, is a 'training bell simulator'. It looks like pit-head winding gear from a colliery, it stands about ten feet tall and it has two exceedingly heavy bell-shaped weights fixed to the wheel on top.

The 'bell' swings full circle like a proper bell in a church tower, you pull it with a proper bell rope and the heavy weights on the 'bell' give it the feel of a true bell. The donging sound comes from a laptop wired up to magnets on the bell wheel.

Option four had come true from my wish list.

The Wombel is made for 'super domestiques'. That's because 'Health & Safety' rules mean it can't be brought into shopping centres via the obvious route. Instead it has to weave through security doors and corridors and car parks – a more challenging route than a Tour de France rider faces when slipping back through the line of support cars to collect fresh water bottles for their team leader.

They made it though, but not without some debate regarding The Wombel's frame and 'Working at Height Regulations'. As Derek said 'I didn't like to tell them we weren't actually at work – work implying some kind of reward. We're retired and we were simply trying to ring a computerised bell simulator in a shopping centre.'

Derek and Ronalda, more than anyone else in the whole of the roller coaster ride of ringing for Le Tour, were the stalwarts, the encouragers, the activists, the anarchists, the cycling converts, the backbone of 'Bell-ringers Herald Cyclists'. Without them, I don't know where we would have been, nor whose sleeve would be on the side of the photo on Bernard Hinault's Twitter profile.

Like the rainy season in the desert, the parched earth of apathy was pushed aside and a new dawn began.

The TV crews rang The Wombel. The radio interviews were in the can and a bell was rung at the launch of the Yorkshire Festival.

Someone else, we know not who, had a toy handbell at the launch too and lost it. It was cared for by Natalie and the team at Welcome to Yorkshire's offices. Under the shadow of Tower Works, a bell was now firmly on the inside track.

Meanwhile, far, far away in Nottingham, a big sigh of relief was heard from an accountant presenting on the strategic imperatives of business case benefits realisation, in an upper room of a popular budget hotel chain.

CHAPTER 18

COMMUNICATIONS – THE SPIDER'S WEB

'Have you thought about having a website, Rod? You've got a lot of news to share. I could help you set it up.'

I am indebted to Bellrope Spider.

We first met, in the virtual world, sometime in the summer of 2013.

There's a long established book called *Dove's Guide for Church Bell Ringers*, commonly known as 'Dove's Guide'. You might have a copy of it. It lists the details, not just of Yorkshire's bells, but of all known rings of bells all across the world – all the bells suitable for change ringing.

Dove had begun tweeting aerial photos of churches in the spring and I was interested to do something similar for the Tour de France route. I just lacked a plane or helicopter or satellite. I was doing pretty well, but these still elude me.

So I decided to phone a friend. Well actually I sent a direct message in Twitter, which led to an email, which led to a phone call, which ultimately led to meeting in the real world when Ros (aka Bellrope Spider) came to Sheffield as guest speaker for the Sheffield University Guild of Change Ringers annual dinner.

As it turned out aerial photos were overtaken by the practicalities of arranging bell-ringing for TV and for the Yorkshire Festival, but Ros was right, I needed a website.

So Mrs Bellsandbikes kindly bought me *Web Design For Dummies* for Christmas and, with three days of intense study of https, cascading style sheets and search engine optimisation, I quickly decided to take Ros's advice and buy an off the shelf website from Wordpress.

Now at this stage I had just changed my Twitter title from @CoverBell to @LeTowerDeFrance and then to @TDF2014Bells and I had determined a strategic next step of rebranding across all channels to @LeTourBellringing.

The name was available online. Should I have been surprised? So I registered it and I paid the premium to avoid uninvited adverts.

Sorted. This was a significant step. However, soon afterwards I reflected on some sensible advice on brand protection. I might want an established and secure brand footprint for myself, but so too do some other organisations. There are some very important and respected brands in cycling. It might be better to avoid any possible misinterpretation of names.

So my second act as a novice webmaster, after purchasing my dotcom address, was to cancel my purchase, unhook my freshly constructed social media hyperlinks and, as quickly as possible, get a new name secured for the site.

Hmm. I had liked @LeTowerDeFrance. I'd liked @TDF2014Bells. But thinking back to Alan's challenge during the Pudsey Bike Ride, how do you keep it simple? And re-useable?

Now then what's this project about?

Bells?

And, er, bikes?

Got it … Bells and Bikes?

Off to Google we go then. A quick search revealed well-trodden ground with 'Bikes and Bells', not surprising perhaps given the merits of a bell on a bike. 'Belles and Bikes' was also widely in vogue for popular women's cycling groups. But 'Bells and Bikes' was unoccupied.

Would Google detect me searching for the name? Would some cheeky squatter spot my search?

Quickly, I registered it. Quickly I rebranded on Wordpress and on Twitter. Quickly I set up a Facebook page. Bells and Bikes was now truly multi-channel, nay omni-channel with my hyperlinks. Bring it on.

With the website in place, it wasn't hard to find content to fill it. Nor to fill the few, spare, waking moments I had left outside of all the other stuff that was going on.

My temptation was to make my website my file of everything I knew about Le Tour Yorkshire, about churches on the route and any other possible links.

That was all very interesting and indeed that was what I did for a couple of months, but as Ros said, it was not that clear for a new visitor to my site.

Something had to change for the audience.

'How about a blog, Rod,' said Ros.

It wasn't easy getting me to understand the difference between a 'page' and a 'post', but I gradually came to see how a rolling news blog on the front page of my site was much easier to follow than updates that could be hidden on any of a dozen pages in the website.

Thank you Ros. Thank you for the many hours you spent reformatting my site, squashing the images to fit the new header and your persistence in diversifying my footprint on the web.

Do pop in. I'm still there. www.bellsandbikes.com ☺

CHAPTER 19

HEADLINERS – THE YORKSHIRE FESTIVAL AND FELLOW ACTS

The build-up to Le Tour was long and eventful. When Dee formally asked for bells on race day, that was after a whole twelve months of trying to get bell-ringers interested. I'd been on tenterhooks, working beyond midnight for a year, but to the outside world you wouldn't know that anything had happened.

Now though, as we entered the actual year of the race, the tempo stepped up a gear. In just a month, bells had gone from a potential sideshow to a headline act.

I was walking to church one Sunday morning when I got the next call from Mark.

'Where would you like to appear on the website?' he asked.

Now, it's not every day that I get a call to ask where would I like to appear on a Tour de France related website. In fairness, though, it was not actually about me – it was 'all about the bell' as they might say – where would I like the bell placing on the map of Festival events?

Well, without wanting to sound immodest, where wouldn't you put the bell? I mean this wasn't just a one-off art installation or a single choir. This was up to forty churches all along the race route.

York? Yes. Leeds? Yes. Holmfirth? Yes. Sheffield? Yes. Blubberhouses? Yes. You name it, bells were there. Urban, rural, hilltop, valley, we had it covered.

'Okay. We'll have the Dales,' I replied. 'Pop the caption in the Dales. There's some great bells there.'

It was also a nice clear space from where the bell could look down on the rest of the Festival map.

Mark returned to what, no doubt, was one of about fifty-two working weekends for the Tour team that year, ensuring Yorkshire was absolutely ready for France.

I carried on to church.

My job that morning, with more than a hint of irony, was to press play on the CD that broadcasts the sound of bells from our church.

No, I'm not proud of that, but we do like the church, it is our local church, and the 'thin' brick walls of the tower would require massive investment to be able to withstand the rotational forces of a set of bells. So off I went to play the CD.

And, as I walked to church, someone in a print room in the Don Valley, with a large pile of yellow card, was typesetting bells into the formal programme book for the festival. Thank you Evolution Print.

Here's what they said.

BELL-RINGERS HERALD CYCLISTS – THE YORKSHIRE ASSOCIATION OF CHANGE RINGERS

There are few sounds as joyful as the peal of bells. The change ringing compositions we hear in this country sound simple but conceal a complex, ever-changing pattern which is uniquely English and is now a specialist art-form kept alive by volunteers. Church bells along the race route will swing into action as the cyclists approach – amplifying Yorkshire's welcome to the racers and celebrating a new festival of ringing.'

Now I've rarely been in this situation before, but when I later received the programme I was ' … oh no …!'

Not in a sense of 'this is wrong' but in a sense of 'I want to go to all these events, but I'm running one myself and I don't have time.'

Oh no!

I was like the proverbial child in a sweet shop.

And it wasn't just that I had a diary clash one weekend. Oh no. Despite the programme highlighting bells for the two days of the race weekend, I was actually trying to organise community events almost every weekend for the whole 100-day festival. And, ahem, I hadn't quite fully explained that to Sally yet.

Sally, of course, was 100 per cent behind my plans, but both of us looked at the adverts for the other events in the Festival and there was just so much we wanted to see.

But we had bells to sort. And day jobs to do. And lawns to mow. And a holiday to take. And shopping to do. But hey, the great thing about jobs like those is 'they'll still be there tomorrow', so yes, we dropped a few. And we planned our calendar for the festival.

In the end, we just never managed to get to a fraction of the events we had hoped to join, but I'd like to share with you a bit about a few of them. In fact, some of them are still there, their legacy remains and you can see them still.

Here are a few of my favourites.

FANTASTICAL CYCLE PARADE – TODMORDEN

Taking up a double page as the first event featured in the programme, the Fantastical Cycle Parade would bring warmth and colour and song and drums and monsters and engineering and, of course, bicycles to the streets of Yorkshire's most famous frontier town, Todmorden.

Bravely located in the demilitarised zone between Yorkshire and Lancashire, this town (sometimes and wrongly thought to be part of Lancashire and certainly on their wish-list of territories to be annexed) is a most beautiful legacy of the era of the mills. I also discovered it to be the gateway to the best kept secret beach in the country – a surreal sandy lake by Stoodley Pike (1,300 feet above sea level) looking down on the Calder Valley.

The parade saw the most amazing range of bicycle creatures, from shimmering fish to great green dragons to pink birds and even a hippopotamus. Local bands, school children, community groups and experienced wheeled animal riders wove through the streets of the town. We watched from a prime vantage point by the roundabout of the A646 and the A6033. I wore polka dots. Our puppet 'Green Guy' wore my Tour de Yorkshire shirt. Grandma took photos and our son, Thomas, relished the wondrous creatures but was a little embarrassed by dad waving that big puppet. Sally had had to give this one a miss. Seeing the photos of the puppetry later on, she confirmed she had made the right decision staying at a safe distance from our antics.

'THE GRAND DEPARTS' – MYTHOLMROYD AND CRAGG VALE

This event was all about cyclists pulling a grand piano up a hill. It was fabulously and imaginatively bonkers and it was the first event where I thought, hey we can gatecrash with bells. I'll tell you more in chapter 24.

GHOST PELOTON

If you saw the Tour opening ceremony, you will have seen some of the Ghost Peloton. If you type Ghost Peloton and Yorkshire Festival 2014 into the search engine of your choice, you can see a whole load more.

My word this was an exciting event. I would have loved to have been able to volunteer for it, just as I would love to have been able to be a Tour Maker, but with bells to organise and indeed bells to ring, I was just never going to have the time for the brilliantly choreographed rehearsals.

But don't let that stop you having a look. We will definitely see more from this event in future.

To quote from the Yorkshire Festival programme:

> *A Ghost Peloton of cyclists, drawing on the spirit of the Tour de France but forsaking dreams of heroism, commits to mass communal movement juxtaposed with complex and extraordinarily athletic choreography inspired by the wheel in motion and performed on film by Phoenix's dancers.*
>
> *Each ghost rider, bike and dancer wears a bespoke LED light suit that changes colour, flash-rate and luminosity as the Peloton changes course. The combined results produce mesmerising light patterns as the cyclists interact with their passing surroundings, culminating in a public performance and film projection as night falls in central Leeds.*

BIKE SHOW – BARNSLEY CIVIC

I lobbied for Barnsley to feature in the Grand Départ. I tweeted my ideas for the route and I tweeted hard, but it didn't make it. It was, therefore, with much excitement and anticipation that I saw Barnsley Civic and its Bike Show in the programme.

We made a family trip to see it with Grandma. Cracking stuff.

You can probably still get a virtual tour of the exhibition if you search Barnsley Bike Show and Yorkshire Festival 2014 on the internet.

I still marvel at one bike in the show which seemed to be all wheels and no frame. Ridiculous or pioneering or both? Will a future time triallist going for the world hour record ever be seen on a version of that machine? I certainly hope so.

FIELDS OF VISION

First there were the Inca lines of Peru in around AD 500. Then the white horse of Yorkshire in 1857. But nothing, nothing, had been done in farmers' fields on quite the scale that Fields of Vision went to, in order to welcome Le Tour.

> *An ambitious land-art project set to appear in the fields and pastures of the South Pennine uplands made by farmers, cyclists and artists.*
>
> *Day Two of the Grand Départ takes the riders through the South Pennine uplands, an area of outstanding moorland and pasture that includes Ilkley Moor. It is here that artists, environmentalists, schoolchildren, hundreds of young farmers and local cyclists will sow, cut and weave original designs into the hillsides and grasslands around the race route.*
>
> *The project brings together commissioned artists working with hundreds of local people to cultivate a patchwork of field-size living installations including three sites designed to grow into natural settings for live performances. These will be animated by music and dancing, curated by arts festivals who are based nearby. This network of locally produced art and reimagined landscape will change and grow over the coming months to form a once-in-a-lifetime experience of the South Pennines.*

TOUR DE FORCE BICYCLE ORCHESTRAS

I was making music *for* the bikes. Huddersfield Contemporary Music Festival (H.C.M.F.) was making music *from* bikes. I would love to have participated. Time conspired against me. I hope that there will be another opportunity.

No self-respecting orchestra should be without its own handlebar trumpet which is why H.C.M.F. are gearing up to help you explore your bicycle's tuneful possibilities and discover new sounds and music composed for hybrid instruments like singing wheels, bicycle thumb pianos and frame harps.

Join H.C.M.F. for one of their free workshops, where you will learn to construct musical instruments from bicycles - as well as how to play them. Taking recycling to a new dimension, H.C.M.F. will help you sonically explore your bicycle and will facilitate the creation of new sounds and music through building instruments from bike parts. No experience or skills needed, just enthusiasm and a sense of adventure.

You will then have the chance to be part of a performance, putting your new skills to the test!

BONJOUR! FILM YOUR TOUR

Here was an event for schools. It wasn't, therefore, going to be something that I could participate in, but you might recall my work colleagues saying that 'Rod never got through a day without mentioning Le Tour.'

Well, nor did some of my suppliers. The daughter of one of the partners of a supplier firm turned out to have made a film at her school that was shortlisted for formal broadcasting on the race day big screens. You can see the film online. The event is now summarised on the festival website as follows:

Bonjour! Film Your Tour was a film competition for schools by Sustrans that promises to take a fresh look at the coming race from the point of view of local children.

Schools across Yorkshire were invited to submit a two-minute film explaining the history, the route, the jerseys, bikes, rules of the race, or what the Grand Depart in Yorkshire meant to them.

The submissions were judged by an independent panel, and then filmed by a professional filmmaker. The resulting film featured six Yorkshire schools and was screened at community cinemas around Yorkshire, as well as on the big screens during the race weekend.

WOOLLY BIKE TRAIL

And last, but by no means least, there was Woolly Bikes. This was an enormous project. It involved ten community workshops all over the county, a vast imagination and the cavernous space of Sheffield Cathedral to bring the whole knitted peloton together at the end.

I've met Cassandra, the event leader, a few times now and like Sharon with her world record bunting, here was an event organiser whose drive, whose leftfield cycling passion and whose community engagement was a constant source of wonder and of encouragement to me as I sought to engage the bell-ringers of Yorkshire, and sometimes of the world.

Cassandra Kilbride is a prolific yarn-stormer. Her crocheted street art makes cheeky visual statements that offer a new reading of the towns and cities we travel through and the monuments and street furniture we pass by. For the Grand Départ, Cassandra is creating ten woolly bikes for a year-long trail connecting ten towns with the many knitters, crocheters and yarn-stormers that have taken part.

Drawing inspiration from iconic Yorkshire themes including the landscape of the Dales, Yorkshire's textile mills, literary heroines and heroes, and the iconic flat cap, each bike gets a woolly makeover using local yarn. Most of the yarn is the produce of Yorkshire sheep, but one special batch comes from a collection of reclaimed saris. The transformed knitted vehicles will go on display in Sheffield this July, before they take up individual positions along the trail route.

Workshops took place between January and June at festivals and venues across the region and were open to anyone with a basic ability of crocheting.

Cassandra's inspiration for Woolly Bikes came from an earlier event, 'Flock to Ossett' in 2012, the essence of which was parades, ukuleles and guerrilla knitting. Trees and lampposts suddenly found themselves wrapped in vibrant woollen coats and a previously anonymous mountain bike had its tubes, its suspension, its wheels, indeed its whole self, dressed in a coat of many colours.

This bike re-emerged in 2013, taking centre stage at the entrance to Welcome to Yorkshire's offices. It was the genesis of Woolly Bikes.

There are many, many more events that I would love to share with you. But I am already over-running on writing the story of the bells, I don't have a publisher yet, I'm way off my plan and so I need to crack on with the bells.

But please do have a look for yourself. There was something for everyone in the 2014 Yorkshire Festival.

And, do you know, it's coming back again. A one-month festival was established as the warm-up to the inaugural 2015 Tour de Yorkshire cycle race and, with significant Arts Council backing, there will continue to be a formal Yorkshire Festival in alternate years starting in 2016.

Website names and references may change, but as mentioned above, you can find a good few films about what happened if you put the event title and Yorkshire Festival into your search engine at home. It might just whet your appetite for more ...

Perhaps you might enjoy watching an event. You might participate in an event. You might even decide that, hey, you could *initiate* an event. Go for it. Vouloir c'est pouvoir. I know because we did it. #bepartofit

CHAPTER 20

MARCH 2014 – DRESS REHEARSAL. BELL-RINGERS HERALD THE BBC TANDEM FOR SPORT RELIEF

In the chill of mid-March, and despite my best endeavours, bell-ringers were still not at fever pitch about the prospect of Le Tour in July. They needed something to cut their teeth on, something to bring it to life.

It was, therefore, with considerable excitement that I got wind of an imminent charity ride of the route.

What happened next was that Harry Gration, Yorkshire icon, he of BBC1 *Grandstand* fame, the celebrity not formerly known as a cyclist, announced that he and fellow BBC *Look North* host, Amy Garcia, would ride the whole of Stages One and Two of Le Tour on a tandem, raising money for Sport Relief.

They decided, or the international cycling authorities told them, I know not which, that they could not ride in the main peloton on race day. So they picked a nice warm week, a bit ahead of the race, giving themselves plenty of time to get round before the Tour motorcade and riders hit our roads.

Their ride would be a great opportunity for us to have a dry run at bell-ringing for televised cycling. So I tipped off a few churches, I tweeted the BBC Tandem Team, and we exchanged a few of those invisible direct message things via Twitter agreeing that a visit to a band of bell-ringers would indeed be of interest to *Look North*. The Tandem Team, of course, had a few other competing offers coming in, and Harry and Amy had a small matter of a 250-mile bike ride to focus their time on too.

However, with the rain falling heavily in Leeds and the snow falling slushily on Holme Moss, the idea of stopping for a cuppa in a nice warm church bell tower must have had some appeal. (Note the subtle bell-ringing pun in there too, a-peal … No? Never mind.)

What Harry and Amy wanted to do was to meet community groups along the way and to share some local stories. We could do that. We could add a bit of music too. So I alerted the churches along the race route and made a few targeted calls.

Harrogate St Peter's was virtually on the finish line of the opening stage of the 2014 Tour, so that seemed like a prime place to focus on, particularly as the Muker to Harrogate leg (day three) of the tandem ride would finish in Harrogate just before Evensong started at St. Peter's.

The riders would be tired, the crew would be hungry, the congregation would be in song and the bells would be a great call to arms for the five days of tandemming ahead of Harry and Amy as they prepared to tackle Stage Two of Le Tour.

Hannah, my contact at St Peter's, got the ringers ready, she pinned mobile numbers on the door to the tower, and the script was ready to formally get the big bells going for the bikes. But the day was cold and the communities along the route had even more stories than could have been imagined. It was too much to fit the bells in as well. The Tandem Team DMd me with sincere apologies

But three days later we nailed it.

I'll let the ringers of Oxenhope and Haworth tell you in their own words.

HARRY AND AMY'S TANDEM TOUR – AN EVERYDAY STORY OF BELL-RINGING FOLK

Wednesday morning isn't the best of times for raising a band at short notice to ring two towers, Haworth and Oxenhope, but we did it. Five of us assembled in the sunshine outside Haworth's door at 9.15 ready for the fray. Look North had been informed and when Pat and I chanced to meet Harry Gration staggering painfully up Main Street from a night's repose at The Fleece, he was well-aware of our intentions. Poor fellow, glad it's him riding the tandem in the full glare of publicity and not me.

A good raise at Haworth led into a steady well-struck 360 of Grandsire, just enough to send them on their way and an excellent lower led by Sue put us into good shape for the mad dash to Oxenhope and meet up with Stuart and Graham. Fortunately we were well enough in time to comfortably raise the bells and watch over the horizon to see the tandemists on their way over Penistone Hill, a mile away.

Now with six of us, we kicked off again with Grandsire, and settled into ringing for as long as necessary to wish Harry and Amy a good journey past all the waving schoolchildren lining Hebden Road, up Charabanc Corner and over Cock Hill. Then after fifteen minutes, the door opened and in came Ian White and cameraman. Wobble, wobble, of course, then 'Bob' and things settled down again as camera came closer, pointed up to ropes and ringers, 'Phew', and on we rang. Then Cameraman decided he wanted a closer view, stepped into rope circle and pointed lens about six inches from Celia's face. 'Rounds.' ... 'Stand!' Hey, ho, another good excuse for failing a quarter, but that would be an untruth.

Watch it on Look North, I hope our one second of fame doesn't include the fire out.

19th March 2014 **Haworth** 360 Grandsire Doubles	1 Sue Burnett 2 Pat Schofield 3 Celia Holmes 4 Andrew Collinson 5 Bob Schofield (Conductor)
19th March 2014 **Oxenhope** 500-ish Grandsire Doubles	1 Stuart Sharp 2 Pat Schofield 3 Celia Holmes 4 Graham Adamson 5 Bob Schofield (Conductor) 6 Andrew Collinson

A fourth tower had also been in the frame, but sadly Skipton, like Harrogate, missed out early in the Tandem Tour. Their ringers eagerly waited a couple of hours for the cyclists, and their ringing would have been joyful for TV, but the challenges of the first day in the saddle and the wealth of welcomes throughout Wharfedale meant Skipton Church could not grace the TV screens that day.

Skipton did, however, come up trumps for Le Tour itself.

The Yorkshire stages of Le Tour were rich with dramatic and emotional pictures of the race and of the crowds. One of the best, of course, being the V-shaped banks of crowds atop Buttertubs which made many a front page and back page in the Sunday papers. As a bell-ringing cyclist, however, few TV images surpassed that of Holy Trinity Skipton boasting a five-metre square yellow jersey hanging from its tower top.

And so, as we concluded our trial run at bell-ringing for a cycling spectacle, we learnt a few things.

Our ringers experienced the satisfaction of success and the angst of a near miss. I was reassured that ringing could indeed be delivered in a manner that was both enjoyable for the ringers and of interest to the outside world and the media. I also confirmed my fear that people don't read their emails. I perhaps needed a new relationship management and communications strategy. Or to actually get out and do some ringing instead of just tweeting about it.

Harry and Amy's ride finished at the English Institute of Sport in the Don Valley in Sheffield. It was firmly imprinted in my diary, but it was a busy week at work and it would be followed by two whole days out the next week – a day filming with BBC *Songs of Praise* in Otley and a day at the Y14 Yorkshire Tourism event in Harrogate. I was not sure that it would be fair to ask Mrs Bellsandbikes and Junior Bellsandbikes how they would feel about me missing tea on Friday night as well in order to watch some more cycling. Nevertheless I chanced my arm and in no time (well actually in suitably safe and speed limit conscious time) I got back from Chesterfield to Sheffield to jump on my bike for the ride across town to the E.I.S. I intended to add to the cheers and show a few polka dots.

I encountered a couple of issues though.

Firstly, I didn't know where the E.I.S. was and I didn't like to admit it. I circled aimlessly around some random car park in Attercliffe for rather too long, before trying a bit further down the road.

Secondly, I might be confident in my spots when I'm the cyclist in a room of suits, but here I was surrounded by the serious race teams of Sheffield. I recognised the shirts and realised I followed a few of them on Twitter.

Their social media timelines were full of professional cyclists they knew and time trials they raced in. Mine, on the contrary, was full of churches and cakes and cows.

They had their carbon frames and aero bars (special handlebars not chocolate bars). I had two pannier bags, trousers tucked into my socks and a full set of mudguards.

They would undoubtedly be faster than me and have more credibility with the TV crew, but let me ask you what really matters on a Friday night? Yes, the takeaway. These riders might look good but they wouldn't be able to pick up a 3, 9, 10, 12, 14, mushroom and cashew nut, and a T11 Kaeng Pad from the New Zing Vaa on their way home and carry it as safely as I would be able to. Oh no. Always take panniers on a Friday.

And after all that, it was my spotty shirt that made it on to the news. Sally and Thomas sat down to watch *Look North* and the exclamation was the inevitable, not for the last time that summer, 'Look at that shirt. Oh, it's dad.'

The Cycle Sheffield campaign team were there too. They gave a rousing roar to the Tandem Team and they knew where to find a good pint afterwards. Mick and Ian kindly invited me to join them, but tea beckoned. I needed to get back for the takeaway.

Harry and Amy raised £139,000 for Sport Relief. You can still donate to their Tandem Tour account on Just Giving or, of course, support the wealth of new fundraisers who inspire us to new levels each year.

I had eventually asked a bloke on a bike for directions on my way to the E.I.S. that evening. It turned out he was 'cycling to work' to help out in a utility company call centre that evening. Sport Relief and similar major fundraising events rely on the goodwill of call centre operators to provide them with the facilities to take telephone donations. That bloke on a bike was going to be on the phone line for Sport Relief that night. Well done, sir. You did a great job. Well done Harry and Amy too.

1 A peloton of accountants on the approach to the Côte de Bradfield on Stage Two of Yorkshire's Grand Départ.

2 Some people I met at the 2007 Tour de France in London.

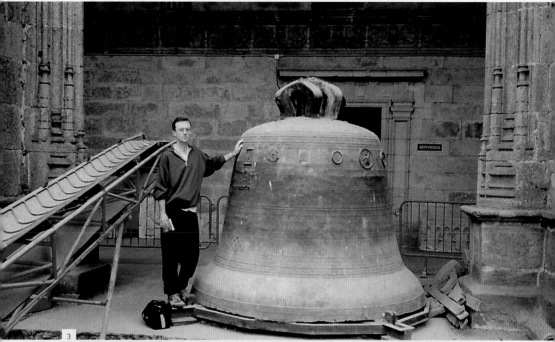

3

4

3 Early symptoms of bells and bikes. With a very large bell in the Catedral de Santiago de Compostela after a 1,000-mile pilgrimage by bike.

4 The hypnotic spiral stairs of Sandal church tower.

5 Sandal church.

6 Thomas has his first go at bell-ringing during Stage Two in York. *Photo courtesy of Peter Bartlett*

7 West Tanfield's bell-ringers were on the big ring a year before the Grand Départ.

5

6

7

8

9

8 Pudsey ears in Paris.
9 Wedding bells, or at least taking photos of street signs related to bells, on our wedding anniversary city break.
10 Church of St Nicholas, Bradfield, from below daffodil height.
11 The assymetrical ears of the Pudsey Bike Ride route planner.
12 Hedge Monster of Cragg Vale.

10

The Post Office

Pudsey Bike Ride

Post Office Riding for Children in Need

11

12

13 The original Woolly Bike in the offices of Welcome to Yorkshire.
14 Handbells on air for BBC Radio Leeds.
15 The Wombel in action at Dewsbury Minster Fest, a fringe event in the Yorkshire Festival.
16 The bird bike of the Todmorden Fantastical Cycle Parade.

15

16

17 Harry Gration and Amy Garcia on the BBC tandem for Sport Relief. A spot of welcome sunshine after riding through snow on the north face of Holme Moss. *Photo with kind permission from Sandie Nicholson, Photos of Yorkshire*

18 Connie Fisher cycles to church in Otley ready to interview me for the BBC *Songs of Praise* Tour de France edition.

19 Car spotting in Harrogate.

20 Oyez oyez. Le Tour is on its way. Thus proclaimed Bridlington Town Crier David Hinde at Y14. World's loudest recorded town crier, 114.8 decibels (Cirrus Research) at Sewerby Hall, Bridlington, Saturday 17 August 2013.

21 Handbells and bikebells on air with Louise Martin on the BBC Radio Leeds Sunday Breakfast Show.
22 Facing the cameras with my hands on the Grand Départ trophy.
23 An early prototype of the South Yorkshire Dry Stone Walling Association's Tour in Dry Stone.
24 All Saints Ecclesall's Cycle to Church Sunday got 209 people on their bikes for Marie Curie.

23

24

25 The bells of All Saints, Cawthorne, featured on the big screen at the Tour opening ceremony.

26 'The Grand Departs' piano pull, with thanks to Dave Nelson composer of the Piano Cycle.
Photo by Sarah Mason Photography, courtesy of Imove Arts and Hebden Bridge Piano Festival

27 On the descent from Worrall to the Côte d'Oughtibridge.

28 Enchanté Monsieur Bernard Hinault. *Photo taken by Peter Dodd on my Blackberry*

29 Northowram bellringers needed a good pie and pint after their exertions. *Photo courtesy of Alan Trebble*

27

28

29

30 They were all pumped up for Le Tour in Leeds.

31 In hindsight people may have thought I was mad. But I was not alone. Thank you Derek and Ronalda Johnstone.

32 Harrogate St Peter's overlooking the finish line of Stage One. *Photo courtesy of Peter Bartlett*

33 The Tour de France on Coney Street York as seen from the roof of St Martin's church.

34 Thomas joins the official Tour Makers. *Photo courtesy of Peter Bartlett*

32

33

34

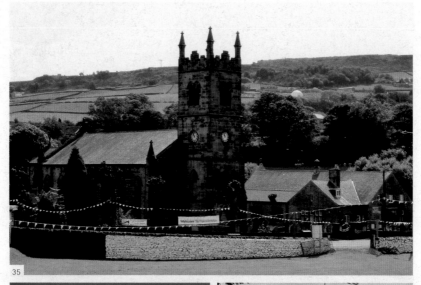

35 St David's Church, Holmbridge, in the foothills of Holme Moss. The venue for a rip-roaring Bells and Bikes charity fundraiser. *Photo courtesy of Ian Gold*

36 The Eiffel Tower of Burley in Wharfedale. *Photo with kind permission from Mike Wild*

37 The tower-topping yellow jersey of Skipton. *Photo courtesy of Chris Wright*

38 Looking down on to the peloton from the top of the tower at East Witton church. *Photo courtesy of Andrew Stockham*

39 Ripon Cathedral in yellow for the 100-Day Dinner. *Photo courtesy of Welcome to Yorkshire*

40 Maillot jaunes in Keighley. *Photo courtesy of Jane Lynch*

38

40

39

41 Honley à la Beatles. The Honley Business Association Committee prepare for Le Tour. *Photo courtesy of Sandie Nicholson*

42 Extourminate extourminate said the Daleks. *Photo courtesy of Chris Sheard, taken at Blackley*

43 Jens Voigt in a swashbuckling breakaway on Stage One as he races past Grinton church.
   Photo courtesy of Lucy McNicholas

44 Skipton from tower top. *Photo courtesy of Chris Wright*

45

46

45 Bank View Café in Langsett does some jolly good cakes. It must have been tempting
to the riders on Stage Two soon after Holme Moss.

46 We rang for the inaugural Tour de Yorkshire in Barnsley. It was bells versus helicopters
in a game of who can make the most noise.

47 After ringing the bell at the 2012 Olympics Sir Bradley chose to cycle past the bells in Barnsley.
Photo courtesy of Mick Greenwood

48

49

48 The Tour de Yorkshire passes Holmfirth church. *Photo with kind permission from Sandie Nicholson*
49 ReCycle Bikes of Sheffield did a splendid job spraying the iconic yellow bikes of the race route.
      Photo courtesy of Angela Walker
50 Bunting in churchyard at Oxenhope. *Photo courtesy of Joanne Holden*
51 Angel bike sculpture in Meltham Post Office in the build up to the 2015 race.

50

51

52 These days bells and bikes are inseparable. Here is 1959 Tour de France stage winner Brian Robinson outside Tideswell church after the bells rang for the Eroica Britannia cycle parade.

53 Cheers.

54 Do you know what Martin. You asked about bells for Le Tour. Well I think we did it.

CHAPTER 21

SONGS OF PRAISE AND THE SONGS TROUSERS

Fans of those Yorkshire celebrities Wallace and Gromit will no doubt be very familiar with *The Wrong Trousers* – robotic leggings that got you dressed faster, hastened breakfast and got you out of the door quickly to resume your search for more Wensleydale cheese. They were, of course, hacked by some evil mastermind who would drag our heroes into the darkest of dangers.

I do not have the 'Wrong Trousers' but I do have the 'Songs Trousers'.

They helped me in my quest for bell-ringing stories in Wensleydale and Wharfedale, and their waistline is nearly as big as that of the gargantuan *Wrong Trousers*.

Putting the similarity of waistline to one side, temporarily, I am glad to say that these trousers did not march me uncontrollably into jewel robberies or other misdemeanours.

They did, however, take me out of my comfort zone and into the lens of a BBC1 camera.

The origin of the Songs Trousers was simply that I had no clothes fit for TV. In fact, I had no clothes fit for a dress down Friday. My usual costume on a Friday being my suit trousers, a smart shirt and no tie. Smart but casual had not found a place in my wardrobe yet. Partly due to time, partly due to low dress standards and partly due to the space required for polka dot cycling shirts and caps. This would not do for TV. Indeed I was specifically advised that polka dots and sponsors logos (even though it was twenty years out of date) would not be permissible. So, a new wardrobe I needed.

The reason I ended up entertaining large waist trousers was directly correlated with the time I was spending writing, emailing and telephoning about bell-ringing for Le Tour. I was doing remarkably little cycling or bell-ringing. But I was able to eat cheese and put on weight.

Dee rang me in early February. 'We're talking to BBC *Songs of Praise* about a Tour de France edition and they are interested in your plans for bells.

Would you mind working up a proposal for a piece on bell-ringing for Le Tour and having a word with their producer?'

Now, at risk of sounding like a broken record, I was beginning to develop a standard response to these kinds of enquiries. It went something like this. Take a deep breath. Pretend not to be wetting yourself with excitement. Do that short punching motion with your forearm that golfers do when they sink a winning putt on the eighteenth green at The Masters. Then politely say 'Wow thanks, I'd love to help. Let me see what I can do.'

My first thought was a bike ride between churches, to take a scenic but achievable section of the race route and ride it with the presenter. In fact, you could do a whole documentary, if not a series, like that, enjoying the scenery, unpacking the heritage of the churches en route, exploring the Christian faith of the bell-ringers along the way and tapping into unexpected French anecdotes throughout the communities on the route.

If you are a TV producer reading this and like the sound of it, you know where I am.

However, for purposes of a half-hour edition of *Songs of Praise*, which would also include a 'best of' compilation of hymns and worship from churches across the county, I needed to produce a more succinct idea.

The answer lay in my Twitter timeline, although it would evolve a bit.

The town of Otley featured loudly in my timeline. I guess one's timeline is only representative of the people you follow, but you only come across people as a result of them having stuff to say. The people of Otley seemed to have an awful lot to say. And it involved a lot of bikes.

In particular, there seemed to be a friendly cycle group, the Otley Social Series, who embraced everyone from semi-pro 'energy bar only' riders to Sunday afternoon 'bring out your cakes' café crawlers. They cycled scenic routes criss-crossing the roads of the Grand Départ and they posted splendid photos of fabulous gateaux at Fewston Church, just off the race route. Here, I was sure, was a story of bikes and churches and with a bit of luck, bells.

So I made a few phone calls and my suspicions were confirmed. What we had was a beautiful little church with great community outreach. It had parish halls that boasted a café much loved by cyclists, it had bell-ringers, it had a vibrant faith journey and to cap it all it had been opened only a couple of years earlier by none other than Monsieur Tour himself, Gary Verity.

It was a short ride from Otley, a town which definitely was on the race route, and which was blessed with another church with bells. Move over J.R.R. Tolkien. Here was a proper Yorkshire story of Two Towers – Lords of the Bell Rings. Here, I thought, was the perfect ride for the programme.

But we mulled it over and it was still a little too complex for the short slot we would get. I needed a shorter option to present to the BBC. At which point one of my favourite stories of the whole 'bells and bikes' journey popped up.

Otley church had been in need of new bell-ringers to reinforce its band. That is a common story across the land. There are just not enough ringers around to keep all the bells going. But Otley had seized on the announcement of Le Tour. In fact, they had managed to recruit a whole new band who were learning especially to be ready to ring for the riders when Le Tour came to town.

Their tower captain, Meg, took my phone call and was absolutely up for the idea of ringing for TV. So too were the band at Fewston. I put them both forward but with the constraints of the slot it had to be just one church. Otley was the one which made the final cut.

I was sad to have to let Fewston know that it would not be them this time, but I was excited to be working with Meg at Otley.

I was also in touch with the Yorkshire Historic Churches Trust, a grant issuing body who were helping many churches and who had approached me early on to seek a link and to let me know about their work helping to fund the recent new church roof at Otley. There truly was a lot to celebrate in Otley.

The date was set for Wednesday 26 March. We would do parallel filming with two BBC film crews; one in Otley and one in the Dales, converging on Ripon Cathedral at the end of the day. I would welcome Connie Fisher, *Songs of Praise* presenter and winner of Andrew Lloyd Webber's *How Do You Solve A Problem Like Maria?* to Otley. We would talk about bell-ringing for the race and Connie would have a go herself under the enthusiastic instruction of Meg. Meanwhile, far away in the north of the Dales, Gary Verity would welcome Claire McCollum to his farm, to meet his flock and to share the story of how Yorkshire won the right to host Le Tour.

The presenters would then ride together into Ripon (perhaps with a bit of help from a car). The day would end with the absolutely monumental 100-Day Dinner in the splendour of Ripon Cathedral – an annual milestone for the Tour organisation bringing together past winners, current teams, dignitaries and Grand Départ hosts.

Footage from the meal featured on the news that evening. It was a wonderful spectacle.

And the bells rang out for it. Ripon's ringers rang a quarter peal of Grandsire Caters before the meal, the cathedral was dressed for Le Tour and France was well and truly here.

Yorkshire Association	1 Anne V. Wood
Ripon, N Yorks	2 Susan E. Welch
Cathedral Church of St Peter and St Wilfrid	3 Janet M. Wadsworth
	4 Rachel Attaway
Thursday, 27 March 2014	5 A. Colin Belsey
1259 Grandsire Caters	6 Martin S. Davies (C)
	7 John R. Welch
Composed by R.W. Diary	8 Wendy Belsey
To mark the start of the 100-Day countdown to Yorkshire's Grand Départ of the Tour de France 2014.	9 Simon D. Ogier
	10 Robert M. Wood
Rung prior to the 100-Days Countdown Dinner held at Ripon Cathedral tonight.	

Meanwhile I was still in Otley. But let me take you back to the start of the day, if I may. It had been an early start that Wednesday.

Otley is the other side of Leeds from me, and Leeds is a good way up the M1, past some particularly popular junctions which you may know from the Radio 2 drive-time playlist. To compound it all, I don't believe in satnav.

It definitely needed an early start. And it needed a bike on the roof.

At one point, the production team had considered whether I might bring a bike for Connie as well as for myself. Mrs Bellsandbikes said, 'Of course you can use my bike for TV' but at the last minute, and probably wisely, the presenters were provided with matching bikes from a local shop.

I would still need my own bike, but it wouldn't get a lot of mileage in. The story of my cycling year really.

It probably did a mile in total. I rode from the car park to the church and back, with a stop in the marketplace and a detour to the post office. But although the mileage was low, it was becoming a pretty experienced TV bike. Having had a camera fixed under its saddle for twenty-five miles for the BBC Children in Need film crew, it would now feature (with its #PudseyBikeRide spotty tape on still) on *Songs of Praise*. I had intended to get polka dot tape on to it by now, but there just hadn't been the time.

I left home at 6.30 a.m. and stopped for a quick tweet at Woolley Edge Services and was soon lost on the Leeds Inner Ring Road. I tried to navigate by the sun, but there wasn't much sun to be seen. I calmed my nerves by listening to Guns'n'Roses very loud. It was probably not a typical warm up for an interview on *Songs of Praise*.

I couldn't get myself on to the Grand Départ route out of Leeds city centre, but eventually somewhere north of town, I found the A659, that nice east-west stretch of the race route from Harewood House to Addingham. I joined it somewhere near Arthington. At last I was on Tour.

I was immediately struck by how much the communities here were 'on Tour' too. Factories had Tour signs up, shops had yellow jerseys and there were no end of farms offering camp sites, parking and festivals.

It was 100 days away, and there was little evidence visible in my home city yet, but it was rockin' for Le Tour on the Otley Road. To be honest, I was a bit emotional driving along it. It was like a homecoming.

I passed dramatic scenery, imposing industrial architecture, a richness of farmland and splendid spires. I took a photo of my bike on my car roof in front of Pool in Wharfedale church under a brilliant blue breakfast sky. This was not one of the Yorkshire Association's 'change ringing' churches, but under Canon Law every church has to have a bell and this photo, months later, went into the Yorkshire Festival summary photo board. It was a fine spire.

It was around 9 a.m. when I reached Otley and I was first there. I hoped I wouldn't be alone.

The good thing was it gave me time for my trademark photo of my polka dot shirt in front of the church tower. And there, where spring had sprung with a flourish, there was an added dimension, rich yellow daffodils all over the churchyard. Daffodils were the logo for Marie Curie Cancer Care, the charity partner of Le Tour Yorkshire. How exactly I was going to support Marie Curie had yet to shape up, but this was a great omen. A pointer to things ahead.

Adrian was next to arrive. He was the soundman. He had a warm, infectious humour and he didn't bat an eyelid as I lay between the gravestones getting the right angle for the photo of my shirt and the tower. Yes it was a first for him, these antics, but no it wasn't out of the ordinary given the diversity of life one encounters as part of an outside broadcast production team.

Next came Reverend Buttanshaw and, yes, he was okay with me pushing my bike into the church and parking it between the pews. He had a busy morning ahead, hosting family groups in the hall and there was a service at 11 a.m. but the congregation was unlikely to fill the whole church on a Wednesday morning and so the bike at the back would probably be okay. All we had to be careful of, was not to ring over the service itself.

Then came Meg.

We'd spoken. We'd emailed. We'd exchanged so many ideas. But we hadn't met.

Now we did. And my word, was she enthusiastic.

So many ideas had been discussed, so much needed doing in the morning ahead, but I could breathe again. We were in safe hands. With Meg, this was going to be a successful shoot.

And so indeed it was.

No one went up in the air. It's a stereotype. A myth.

No one complained about the noise. The town was excited about the bells.

And our presenter learnt to ring. Well, a bit. Under good supervision.

However, I fluffed my lines when it came to the interview. Everyone said it came out well on TV, but I was annoyed with myself. I blanked in front of the camera. I love presenting to big audiences, I love the cut and thrust of open forum Q&A, but for the first time on film I blanked. There was so much I wanted to say, so much more to celebrate, but in the thirty-second soundbite, yes, I guess it was okay actually. Miracles of the editing suite.

I learnt from it though, I can tell you. BBC Radios Leeds and York got it full on the next day. My word I enjoyed those radio interviews on the Thursday. You have to take the knocks, ride with it and get back in the saddle. I was on a roll now.

In hindsight I realise there was no make-up room. I don't get to see the top of my head very often, but the great thing about being filmed from above as you climb a spiral staircase, is that you do get to see, on TV, whether or not you have a bald patch. I am now clear that I do indeed have a slight hair loss issue and perhaps next time I could get a bit of mascara or something on that shiny patch. Just an idea.

Anyway, we had a fine time with the film crew. Connie, Judith, Adrian and Tom. Really nice folk to work with as were Mel and Lizz, the producers.

And what a nice band of ringers too at Otley. It was a pleasure to meet them and share their story – a band inspired by Le Tour. A band inspired to spend a year learning a new art, to be ready with a big loud Yorkshire welcome for the riders of Le Tour de France.

The programme was broadcast on Sunday 29 June, the weekend before the Grand Départ. The bell-ringing extract remained on the iPlayer longer than some chart topping soaps. Have a look, it may still be there.

CHAPTER 22

Y14 – HANDS ON THE TROPHY

The 100-Day dinner in Ripon had been the curtain raiser for the final countdown to Le Tour.

It was followed, on Thursday 27 March, by the ticker tape launch of the 100-Day Yorkshire Festival at the annual Yorkshire Tourism event, this year branded Y14.

The venue was Harrogate International Conference Centre, the audience was the world and the front row included Monsieur Bernard Hinault.

Nick Clegg, Deputy Prime Minister, took the stage as the day kicked off and the breakfast show audiences of BBC Leeds and York got a taste of the church bell-ringing to come.

I arrived by train.

Not for the first time, nor the last, I was the only passenger on the Sheffield-Barnsley-Leeds section wearing a king of the mountains cycle shirt. You may be astonished to know that I was still the only polka dot passenger on the next train too, a train which started a matter of yards from the upcoming Grand Départ ceremonial start line in Leeds and terminated a couple of pelotons away from the finishing line of Stage One in Harrogate.

I am pretty sure that other people do wear these shirts. There are many good reasons to do so.

Firstly, they are very comfortable. Not necessarily easy on the eye of your fellow passengers, but very comfortable in themselves as a garment. Particularly in the larger sizes. I tend to find, as a commuter, that I don't need them to be too aerodynamically tight fitting for every day trainwear.

Secondly, they have lots of handy storage compartments. Three good-sized pockets on the back, ideal for the suite of cameras, phones and notebooks that any self-respecting Tour de France addict has with them on a day out in Harrogate.

Finally, and something that they don't always say during Paris Fashion Week, the big red spots provide ample disguise for tomato ketchup stains if you have an incident while eating fish and chips.

For all these reasons, I truly am convinced that other people do wear these shirts. It's just that the wearers seem exclusively to be either racing in Le Tour de France, standing in a bar watching Le Tour de France, or jumping up and down for TV cameras roadside on a stage of Le Tour de France.

If you see anyone in polka dots on the Barnsley train, fair bet it'll be me. Hello.

So here I was, wearing big red spots, stepping out on to a wet platform under heavy grey skies in Harrogate. It was the sort of weather that had graced many a 'prologue' to Le Tour, a 'prologue' being the short individual time trial that often takes place on the first Saturday of the race. Wet prologues had brought much excitement and much drama, including nasty falls for some much-loved Tour riders. One of the most notable being in 1995 when stage favourite, Chris Boardman, slipped on wet tarmac followed by the ignominy of being hit by his own team car, as it too suffered on the slippy surface. For my part, I stepped down safely on to the terra firma of Harrogate.

I don't know about you, but I always have a tinge of satisfaction whenever I safely step off the train on to the platform. Mind the gap. Make the plunge. One small step for a man, one giant step for bell-ringers on the way to Le Tour.

And 'alors' what did I see down the platform? What did I see on the skyline as the railway tracks curved east out of Harrogate? Ah, yes a church spire! Incroyable! Merveilleux! The French visitors would see that too when they arrived in July. Churches were already dominating the landscape. Bring it on.

I didn't know Harrogate then. I do now. I even managed, by amazing coincidence, to get placed at Harrogate Post Office as a Christmas Maker later that same year. I got the chance, on my walk to work, to see the huge Tour photo galleries that were still gracing the shop windows five months after the race had moved on. The yellow jerseys were still there, the carved tree on The Stray still stood as a bold monument to the race, and Cav's cycling shirts looked well on the walls in The Cavendish Arms.

It was well worth a pint (after work, let me be clear), to enjoy the atmosphere, to read the storyboards on the tables, to get a selfie by the shirts and to take yourself back to the summer of 2014.

I'd been in dialogue with bell-ringers in Harrogate for some time, as I mentioned before. So, despite shivering in the cold and wet of a March morning, I had a warm feeling about the town.

I was also, as you know, in polka dots and I was snap happy.

The tourist information centre wasn't open at the hour I arrived, but I was able to enjoy a great cycling display in its window. And then, a few yards away across the road, I got my first glimpse of the Tour de France lead car on Yorkshire soil.

Whether or not 'it's all about the bike', to reference a famous book title, there's a bit of the race that is all about the car. If you have ever watched Le Tour you are likely to have developed some form of affinity with the wonderful red lead-out cars, presently Skoda, which run just ahead of the riders. The occupants have the most amazing view on to the front of the peloton and by their arm gestures on TV they somehow transmit an extra emotion to the viewer, to draw you into the race, to imagine you are there. These cars have open roofs enabling the two rear passengers to stand, calmly or animatedly, cheering and greeting the riders and the fans.

And thus I found myself cheering a car in Harrogate.

A passer-by agreed to stand and get wet by the car too, kindly putting her brolly down for a moment to take a photo of me by this magnificent automobile.

But I was really in Harrogate for a conference, not for a car, so I wiped the rain off my camera screen, shook myself like a dog climbing out of a lake and made my way to the doors of the conference centre.

I'd been asked to turn up early for Y14 so that I could be interviewed on the BBC Leeds Breakfast Show. They were running a big series in the lead up to the Grand Départ – '100 Days, 100 Stories' and church bell-ringing was one of those stories.

Bells were capturing the imagination of the media. This was a great PR opportunity to attract new recruits. However, it was not without collateral damage in the bell-ringing fraternity.

The thing was that, like most clubs and societies or even businesses, the family of bell-ringing embraced a wide spectrum of people and opinions. Not everyone likes change and, understandably, not everyone welcomed my onslaught of emails and phone calls to corral a county into ringing for a bike race.

The Facebook groups for bell-ringers were already a heated debating chamber between groups with different opinions about publicity, recruitment and community engagement. As I bulldozed my project through, I found I was simultaneously the fresh story on the block as well as the new target in the crossfire.

Some ringers liked things as they were, the number of ringers might be in decline but it was what it was and the best thing was to carry on doing your very best in the way you have always done. Some other people wanted radical change, they wanted a repositioning of the public stereotypes of bell-ringers, they wanted a positive social media story and they wanted fresh new recruits.

Some folk wanted to work together and reach a consensus for progress. Others wanted to take the glory for no work.

I was a Tour de France addict, with an absolute conviction that Le Tour was something we should celebrate and something that we should seek a legacy from.

I'm not sure how to present this in Venn diagram format. To be honest I may not even need to. But I did often think about it. I don't know how much I represented the voice of change or how much I was an irritating geek in spots who tweeted a lot about bells but didn't do enough actual ringing.

I knew I needed to do more ringing, and indeed I wanted to, but it just hadn't fitted with work, church and home for the last few years. I'd spent too long on trains from London, my priority was 'bath, book and bed' with our son Thomas once I got home, and on a Sunday we were enjoying the fellowship of a church which ironically did not have a set of bells. There was precious little time left for bell-ringing practise nights.

That being said, representatives of the Central Council of Church Bell Ringers indicated their support for what I was doing.

I, therefore, walked through the doors of Y14 knowing that I was speaking with a mandate from the ringing world.

I didn't get far.

BBC Radio York had secured the lobby area.

'Ah, you look like a cyclist. What's your role here? Would you mind doing an interview with Jon Cowap. You'll be on air in five minutes. Stand over there please.'

Er, okay. I'm on my way to BBC Leeds though. I'm booked for an early interview.'

'Great. They won't mind.'

On 27 March 2014, for the breakfast-show audiences of Yorkshire, church bell-ringing was the prize scoop.

Gary Verity walked past.

'Hi Gary. We had a great day with the *Songs of Praise* team in Otley yesterday. How about you?'

'Hi Rod, great to see you. Yes a very good day,' he replied with a smile, swept along by his communications team, come bodyguards, on the way to his next TV interview. Few Yorkshire folk, outside of newsreaders and weather hosts, had more airtime that year than Gary. Few, certainly, had such a story of vision, community and global unity to share.

The interview with BBC York went well – no lost words, no camera fright, the story was clear now. I am convinced there was something soothing about that great big soft radio microphone that engendered a spirit of confidence and ownership that the TV camera lens had not as easily matched. Although in time it would.

'Yes, that is indeed a cycling shirt I am wearing. The King of the Mountains top. Purchased in France, on the Champs-Élysées, yards away from the finish line of the 1992 Tour de France.'

'Why bell-ringing?'

'Well, why wouldn't you want to welcome the world's biggest annual sporting event with the world's largest and loudest musical instruments?'

'Cow bells are great on the Alpine climbs, but wait 'til you hear church bells for the race in Ilkley, Otley and West Tanfield.'

We talked about the Yorkshire Festival and the exciting events people could participate in; we talked about the impact Yorkshire churches would have as focal points for the TV cameras in the helicopters and we talked about the Yorkshire Association of Change Ringers having hundreds of churches all across the county, not just on the race route. All those churches were keen for new recruits, I said. We need to ensure we have enough ringers to keep the bells going for the weddings of generations yet to be born.

Polka dots, as I think I have said before, give you an appearance, and indeed a feeling, of authority. People look to you as someone who must know about pro-cycling.

The fact is, a Barnsley fan in a Barnsley shirt, would indeed have an encyclopaedic grip of the stats and fixtures of football. I, however, had some notable gaps in my record keeping on cycling. But what I lack in statistics, I cover with passion and enthusiasm for the landscape of the sport of cycling and the excitement of the roadside spectator. I could talk for England. Or, being a bit biased, I could talk for Yorkshire.

And I did.

The listeners of BBC Leeds got it all again too. I enjoyed it. I hope they did too. Tour reporter, Richard Edwards, was certainly an enthusiast. Thanks for the interview.

Suitably energised, I then 'calmly' worked the room.

I found out about a growing Yorkshire business at a stand over there, I bought my Yorkshire Grand Départ shirt and flask at the stall in the centre, and yes I grabbed a few freebies in the other aisles. All the while giving an understated, pleasant nod to anyone looking at me out of the corner of their eye and thinking 'I don't recognise that bloke in spots as a Tour rider, but I'm not sure.'

I left them to ponder it.

The Seabrooks crisps had all been eaten by the more overstated guests of Y14 by the time I got to their stand. I love Seabrooks crisps. It's the crinkles. It's the texture. It's the taste. Their brand also offered me the only six-pack I would get that year. I had little time for exercise during my campaign, but I had much time for six-packs of crisps as I sat typing the next press release.

Lottie Shaw did, however, have some edible merchandise left – Yorkshire parkin. Splendid. And cycling mugs. Even better. But alas the pockets on my cycle shirt eventually reached their limit. This was like Christmas shopping, but tastier. I do recommend Lottie Shaw's parkin.

And so, after a busy morning of networking, broadcasting and eating, the time came for the main event – the showcase launch of the 100-Days in the main theatre of the conference centre.

I'd not been to a 'tourism' led event before. I'd never thought it was relevant to me, I hadn't felt the personal or business need and, of course, there was always a more urgent priority at work to deal with. How wrong I'd been.

I've been to, and hosted, no end of internal business conferences before. I've happily held the stage, talking enthusiastically about the customer and about the role of finance in corporate transformation.

But within all of us, there is a need for something beyond work. Or if there isn't then there should be. There is a deeper need for belonging, a need for a role, a need to be recognised within your tribe. It might be driven by Scottishness, Essex or football. For me it was Yorkshireness. And here, at the Yorkshire Y14 event, we had the slickest multi-media presentation I'd ever seen bringing our county, our story and our ambition together. It included the very footage that had captured the hearts and minds of the ASO in Paris and had secured the hosting of Le Tour. It captured the hearts and minds of everyone in the theatre in Harrogate.

The rugged splendour of the moorlands, the passion of the people and a cheeky clip of Mark Cavendish extolling Yorkshire to Christian Prudhomme. I say cheeky because it had been played to Christian unexpectedly one day on a vast city centre TV screen; a day when he was walking through Leeds during the assessment phase of the various bids to host the 2014 Tour.

It was a great film. It was inspiring. And it lifted our commitment to the festival and to Le Tour to an even higher level. We all shared Gary's commitment to make this the grandest Grand Départ ever.

We were treated to a mini rock concert, top sports interviews, highlights of the year past and an introduction to Martin Green, MC of the London 2012 opening ceremony.

The main event culminated in a very excited and surprisingly orderly queue to get your photo taken with the Tour de France Grand Départ trophy.

In the mêlée to get to the queue, I politely accosted Martin to tell him about churches and to give him my 'Tour bells' business card. I then took a photo of the seat that Bernard Hinault had sat in, as you do, before bumping into Sharon for a further inspiring update on the world record bunting project. She didn't need a photo of Bernard's seat. She'd been in the Tour de France lead car on Cragg Vale with him the day before. 2014 was a truly remarkable year where we really got to the heart of this global event and where we were able to mix, in the most remarkably relaxed environment, with icons of the sporting world. I can't wait for Le Tour to come back again.

All in all, 26 and 27 March 2014 were two very good days. Just what I needed as an antidote to the upcoming financial year end back at work. Oh to be an accountant.

CHAPTER 23

ON AIR NEXT – YORKSHIRE RINGS OUT ACROSS THE WORLD

When I started writing this book, I had some very clear ideas about how it would be structured. There would be forty-two chapters, twice the number of stages in Le Tour and twice the number of 'virages' (hairpin bends) on that most famous of Tour climbs, Alpe d'Huez.

There would be twenty-one chapters for the build-up to the summer of 2014 and there would be twenty-one chapters on the actual delivery of events for the Yorkshire Festival and for Le Tour.

In time, it morphed into the themes you now see, but nevertheless I was reassured from the outset that I had ample topics across 2013 and 2014 to differentiate so many chapters.

However, despite my 'clarity' of the high level map of the book, I didn't have a firm sense of the detailed directions I would take as I wove through the sub-themes within each chapter. I kind of found my pen taking me in unexpected, but hopefully relevant, directions as I wrote.

It was the same with my ideas list for how bells would connect with Le Tour.

Back in January 2013, I'd written my first list of things that bell-ringers could possibly do.

One of those was an idea called 'Ringing Yorkshire Across The World'.

What I meant by that was for the 'method' Yorkshire to be rung as far and wide as possible. Yorkshire, of course, being one of the most common and most popular methods around. I included the diagram for it in chapter 5.

My idea was to try to find willing bands across Yorkshire and across the UK, but also across the world, who might ring this method and who might dedicate their performance to Le Tour in Yorkshire. Now there were a couple of issues with that. Firstly, I'd been ringing so little recently that some of my own county ringers had forgotten who I was. In consequence, the likelihood of me readily connecting with a UK ringer who might be happy to introduce me to their friends abroad was somewhat small. The second issue, should I find a friendly contact abroad, was that they were unlikely to be Tour de France addicts. Why then should I expect a band of bell-ringers on the opposite side of the world to dedicate their valuable time to a bike race in the Yorkshire Dales?

Nevertheless, I like to be optimistic. So I initiated a few cold calls and emails.

Those didn't take me far, but bizarrely one evening I found myself on Facebook wherein appeared a credible lead. I say bizarrely because I am much more comfortable on Twitter, but needs must, so I had gone googling or searching or whatever it is you do on Facebook and, would you know it, something cropped up.

It seemed that a young ringer from London had recently moved to Australia. A bit more searching revealed the names of some churches with bells and indeed some ringers down under. And then, without warning, Matthew Sorrell, President of the Australia and New Zealand Association of Bell-ringers (ANZAB) flashed across my screen. And something about a bike,

Now I might have got this wrong, and I really am hesitant about cold calls, but I facebooked him and lo and behold he was aware of my project, he had a band who would be happy to ring with us and he had an interest in cycling.

I mentioned this to Richard Edwards at Y14 during my interview on BBC Leeds. I mentioned the possibility of ringing Yorkshire in Australia. I also had a tentative lead in New York too.

'Right,' said Rich, 'better get his number. This would work well on Liz Green Live'.

Liz Green hosted the weekday Breakfast Show and the '100-Days, 100 Stories'. Bells from Australia would be brilliant.

I put Matthew and Rich in touch, and in no time we had a booking for an 8 a.m. live interview, 8 a.m. GMT being teatime in Adelaide.

Matthew went above and beyond, or whatever you do when you are down under. Here is the interview, starting with Liz introducing Matthew to the listeners of West Yorkshire:

'We celebrate the Tour de France by ringing out church bells, not just here, but in Australia too … (Liz then played a recording of bells) … I think that is one of the most glorious sounds on Earth,' she said.

'The ringing of the church bells. Now, during the Tour de France '100-Days, 100 Stories', here on your station for the Tour de France, when it's taking place in July, Yorkshire-based church bell-ringers will get our church towers pealing away. However, get this, 9,000 miles away in Perth, Western Australia, in support, bell-ringing across the globe, they are going to be doing the same. Let's cross now to Matthew Sorrell, President of the Australia and New Zealand Association of Bell-ringers. He is talking to us from his church in Perth.'

'Good morning Matthew,' said Liz.

'G'day Liz,' he replied enthusiastically. 'I am actually in Adelaide here in Australia.'

'How lovely. How lovely and how lovely to talk to you. Thank you for ringing your bells for the Tour de France.'

'My pleasure. Adelaide is actually the home of the Pro-Tour Opening Inaugural Event every year, the Tour Down Under, so we have a pretty good idea about what you are going to experience and it is just quite fantastic.'

'It is,' said Liz, 'but to actually take the time and the trouble to ring those bells for Yorkshire, even with that link, I know this all happened via Facebook, I just think it's exceptional. You must just really love and appreciate what we are doing with the Grand Départ here in Yorkshire, in West Yorkshire.'

'Well look it's just terrific,' he replied, 'and, if I can, I'd love to do a Bradley Wiggins for you. You might remember he opened the 2012 Olympic Games with a twenty-three-tonne bell. I've got a two-kilogramme bell here which I can ring for you (ding ding ding ding) to celebrate Yorkshire and the Grand Départ of Le Tour de France in Yorkshire. Fantastic.'

'Thank you so much,' said Liz. 'That's a big bell you've just rung for us in Yorkshire.'

'As it turns out,' replied Matthew, 'this one is the trophy for the winners of the International Bell-ringing Competition, held about twenty-five years ago. We hold that proudly, here in Adelaide.'

Liz was in raptures. 'Well, I am in awe. I am so grateful that you are prepared to do that for us. And you will ring your bells at the same time that the bells ring across this county, will you?'

'That's exactly right,' Matthew affirmed, 'and, in fact, the Perth bell-ringers will be going to York. Now that's not your York. It's actually a township about sixty miles east of Perth that has a bell tower. So, appropriately, the bell-ringers of Perth will be in York just for you.'

'Thank you, may I ask you Matthew, in Adelaide, live on Breakfast across West Yorkshire this morning. We are proud to be Yorkshire. We are proud of the Tour de France 100-Days, 100 Stories. Matthew, could you ring that bell again?'

'I could do that for you, certainly. Here we go,' came the reply. Ding, ding, ding, ding, ding, ding.

'Matthew Sorrell, thank you. President of the Australia and New Zealand Association of Bell-ringers, live in Adelaide, for the Breakfast Show here at BBC Radio Leeds. And those bells, down under, in the Antipodes will ring at the same time as our Yorkshire church bells when the Tour de France begins in July. How amazing is that? Matthew, thank you, Matthew we appreciate it. Ring a ding, as we hold hands across the globe in celebration.'

Brilliant. Bells in Yorkshire and bells in Australia. Both in York. Ringing Yorkshire.

Fittingly, Matthew also emailed us a selfie which joyously came through upside down just as we imagine photos from Australia always should.

Bell-ringing doesn't get better than this. Except when the bell-ringers of Holy Trinity, Wall Street, New York delivered the third York.

The icing on the cake was a total surprise to me. It wasn't a York, but it was a peal of Yorkshire rung in Holland in a place called Dordrecht, about an hour away from the start point of the 2015 Tour de France in Utrecht. I had no idea there were bells hung for English Change Ringing in Holland. Sheffield Cathedral bell-ringers had better knowledge than me though. Theirs was the fourth ring of Yorkshire truly taking us global and, better still, laying a link to keep the flame burning into the following year's Tour too.

Here are the records of all four performances and the ringers involved. Yorkshire salutes you all.

Yorkshire in York, Australia
Holy Trinity, York

Saturday 5 July

1280 Yorkshire Surprise Major

1 Debbie Hay
2 Richard Offen (C)
3 Andrew Baxter
4 Callum Crofton
5 Tony Godber
6 Ron Chapman
7 Bert Woolven
8 Adam Beer

By ANZAB ringers

Yorkshire in New York, USA
Trinity Church, Manhattan

Sunday 6 July

1250 Yorkshire S Major

1 Tina Hitchings
2 J. Caroline Flockton
3 Stuart J. Flockton
4 John Hitchings
5 Jennifer S. Mackley
6 Jeremy C. Bates
7 Robert J. Flockton
8 Duncan J. Large (C)

By New York ringers

Yorkshire in Dordrecht, Holland
Dordrecht, 't Klockhuys

Friday 4 July

5088 Yorkshire Surprise Major

1 Simon J. Reading
2 Chris Bostock
3 Gail L. Randall
4 Paul M. de Kok
5 Richard F. Knights
6 Andy P. Thackeray
7 Harm Jan A. de Kok
8 Peter C. Randall (C)

By Yorkshire Association ringers

Ringing for the riders on Stage Two
York Minster, North Yorkshire

Sunday 6 July

1313 Stedman Cinques

1 Jonathan J.F. Stokoe
2 Helen M. Beaumont
3 Alice A. Longden
4 Sophie E. Palmer
5 Peter D. Hughes
6 Christopher S. Caryer
7 Christine B. Potter
8 Simon A. Percy
9 Peter J. Sanderson (C)
10 David E. Potter
11 David R. Mitchell
12 Christopher D. Young

Rung through the start of Stage Two
of the Tour de France in York.

With the global ringing and with Matthew's interview the bar had moved up several notches for what we now expected from bell-ringing. The media wanted more and I was up for the next challenge.

The BBC French Service sounded like a great opportunity. Welcome to Yorkshire's London press agency, Cornershop, rang me to ask if I could give an interview in French as part of an English culture programme on the French Service. They said that the reporter was somewhere in Yorkshire. They should have perhaps added a few *peut-etres*, an enigmatic shrug and a Gallic wave of the hand though to indicate a certain fluidity to the timing of the interview. The reporter had been at the 100-Day dinner but had subsequently gone A.W.O.L. Perhaps he had been overcome by the scenery. Perhaps he had overeaten. Perhaps he had discovered the breweries of Masham just up from Ripon. Whatever the reality, I cleared my diary for early Friday afternoon, took my dictionary into a quiet room at work and waited for the call. It never came. Not from him, nor from Missing Persons at Interpol. I hope he made it home okay.

Sadly that was the interview that got away. France missed out on an update on bell-ringing but the students may, in fairness, have benefitted from avoiding my Yorkshire French accent.

The next interview nearly slipped through my fingers too.

Welcome to Yorkshire had two press agencies on the case and it was Anita Morris Associates, the northern agency, who called me next. They had an enquiry from the BBC Leeds Sunday Breakfast Show. Could I make it into the studio for 7 a.m?

Now I have to say, not for the first time, how understanding Mrs Bellsandbikes was. My crime this time was to stay up until 2 a.m. Saturday night writing an article for *The Ringing World* newspaper about *Songs of Praise* and 'The Grand Departs' (see next chapter) and then get up only three hours later to drive to Leeds. I was totally alert. I was on rich adrenaline. No need for E.P.O. or other banned substances. I was on a Tour high.

But there were two issues in Leeds, firstly, the road routing is a nonsense. I got lost so many times trying to find a road to a car park anywhere near the studio. Then I got trapped in my car.

I don't know what I did. I must have leaned against those buttons on the door that lock your car doors while you are still inside. I don't know. I didn't hear anything click. But whatever happened I found myself helplessly tugging at my door handle and unable to get out.

It went on for what seemed an eternity. I even started trying to phone the studio but I was shaking so much by then that I couldn't unlock my phone either. Argh! Trapped in a car park outside the studio. Due on air in ten minutes and no idea how to get out. This was very embarrassing.

I'm not sure how I did eventually get out. I had thrown my keys to the floor in anger, which was quite a feat in itself given the confined space and lack of headroom to do an actual overarm bowling motion. But whatever it was, something clicked and suddenly the door handles worked again. I was free.

It might have been less stressful to have cycled up the M1 for the interview. Perhaps Gary Verity could call in a favour and get me a motorbike escort for the ride next time? Anyway, I escaped the car, found the studio entrance and stood in awe of the photo board in reception, Harry Gration and Amy Garcia of the BBC Tandem Team, plus all the rest of the BBC *Look North* and BBC Leeds Team, they were all there. TV icons. Radio icons. But they weren't in the office. Sensible really at that time of day. I hoped they hadn't locked themselves in their cars too.

I chatted with the minister and the rabbi who were on before me. They were regulars and were here to review the Sunday papers. The microphones held no fear for them. But the microphones did something for me. Their colours were, get this, red, yellow and green.

Can you believe it?

'Believe what?' I hear you say.

Well, believe that the microphones were the same colours as the leaders' jerseys of Le Tour de France?

Getting access to the studio to grab a photo was kind of okay. I didn't interrupt the 9 a.m. host too much as he prepared his script. The mikes made a nice tweet. If you like bikes, of course.

And the interview went well. We talked about the usual stuff, bells, bikes and spotty shirts, but it was also the day after 'The Grand Departs' and Louise Martin who hosted the show was well up on the previous day's antics of a grand piano being pulled up Cragg Vale by bikes. We talked about how we rang the bells for it. More to follow in the next chapter.

I also took a ragbag of handbells and a bike bell into the studio. It's hard to fit a church bell in your bag for a broadcast, but a bike bell was okay and I happened to have a bag of assorted handbells that had been found in the vestry of our church.

There wasn't a complete octave and real handbell ringers would be shocked by them, but four of them, chosen carefully, made quite a nice sound. A nice little taster for the Leeds audience.

I was out of the studio by eight. I'd have been home by nine if I hadn't wandered off to take photos of my shirt outside St Anne's Cathedral, Leeds Minster and the Tower Works. As it was, I did wander off and I was more than a little late home. But Sally and Thomas had listened online, enjoyed the show and all was well.

Life on air was good.

I just did one more interview that year. BBC Leeds asked for one the day before the opening ceremony. I couldn't get to Leeds so I popped into Radio Sheffield. I sat in their guest studio ringing handbells for the people of Leeds again while Toby Foster and the Radio Sheffield Breakfast crew sat next door talking about Le Tour to the good folk of Sheffield.

The airwaves were rich with bikes and bells. You can probably get some of it online still.

And I'm happy to say that BBC Radio in Yorkshire still seem to have red, green and yellow furry microphones a year after Le Tour.

The Tour de France certainly left its mark on air in Yorkshire.

CHAPTER 24

APRIL 2014 – IN TUNE WITH 'THE GRAND DEPARTS'

There have been many iconic partnerships in the history of this blessed county.

In cricket we had Sutcliffe and Holmes, formidable opening bats for Yorkshire around 1920. In television we had Compo, Clegg and Foggy. Okay that was three of them, but fine partners nonetheless. And in transport who can forget the A1/M1 interchange.

In April 2014, however, the time was ripe for bells and pianos.

Bells and bikes had already raised enough eyebrows and disproved the doubters.

With the advent of the Yorkshire Festival though, it was time for a new phase of celebrating Le Tour. A pioneering experiment in fusion percussion was born.

The genesis of my idea was a separate Act in the Festival, 'The Grand Departs'.

This event, among many great acts, was the one that most captured my imagination when I first read the programme for the Festival. I'll let them introduce themselves in their own words.

> How many cyclists does it take to pull a piano up the longest continuous hill in England? Is it even possible?
>
> With the Grand Départ of the 2014 Tour de France taking place in Yorkshire, these were the questions Hebden Bridge Piano Festival and Imove wanted to answer.
>
> Whilst our director Dave Nelson set about composing new piano music to be played throughout the climb by local, regional and international pianists, sculptor/engineer Andy Plant was brought on board to design and build a bespoke vehicle called the PianoPorté to carry the piano, and to be propelled by, after much consideration, a total of 18 cyclists.

By this time, we had begun a 100-day planner for our calendar at home and 5 April was quickly marked down for a family outing to see the piano pull. I had, of course, become reasonably well-acquainted with Cragg Vale by now and I was excited by the wonderful absurdity of the planned performance. It was a worthy climb for a team of cyclists, let alone eighteen amateurs bolted together pulling a grand piano.

Now then, aren't there some bells at the bottom of Cragg Vale? Isn't there a tall tower atop a certain church by the name of St Michael's overlooking the bridge on the turn at the foot of the climb?

Well, do you know, yes there is.

So I sent a direct message to the Hebden Bridge International Piano Festival Team, the masterminds behind 'The Grand Departs'.

'Hi. We may be able to ring Mytholmroyd bells before u set off up Cragg Vale – to celebrate your project. Would that be ok? – Rod?'

That same evening, the reply came straight back.

'Wow, that sounds brilliant. Dave Nelson will give you a call! ☺ thank you'

Dave, it transpired, was composing the opening piece for 'The Grand Departs'. It was a piece to be played by none other than Kathryn Stott, renowned international concert pianist.

Kathryn Stott is internationally recognised as one of Britain's most versatile and imaginative musicians and among today's most engaging pianists. She is in demand for a wide variety of chamber music alliances, playing with some of the world's leading instrumentalists, as well as appearing on major international concert platforms in recitals and concerto performances. Kathryn has also directed several distinctive concert series and festivals and has developed an extensive and exceptionally varied catalogue of recordings.

Kathryn, as her website says, was born in Lancashire, but every story has a happy ending and she is now a proud resident of Hebden Bridge, Yorkshire.

'What key is the piece in, Dave? Mytholmroyd bells are in F.'

'It's in F.'

Now you couldn't have made this up.

One of the world's leading exponents of the piano would be launching her festival performance in F, and our bells were in exactly the same key.

If I could just get a band of ringers together, we were set for a fantastic duet. Well, actually a nine-et or whatever you call eight bells and a piano.

There was just the slight issue that Mytholmroyd needed some new ringers to make up their band, I didn't personally know the existing band and the other likely locals who could help were on a coach trip to Blackpool or somewhere far afield that day.

I was, however, knee deep in last minute, seat of the pants planning by this point. Committing to a duet or nine-et with a global star was of little additional worry given that I'd already committed to the world's biggest annual sporting event that I'd get the bells of the county ringing, despite only two or three replies from towers in six months.

'Oh yes Dave. We'll sort this.'

The first contact I had with Mytholmroyd had actually been in the preceding November. It was a call both rich with anticipation of a festival of Frenchness and yet full of unexpected sadness. Julia, whom I called, was so excited that Le Tour was coming to town. She and her husband had lived in Paris, of all places, for many years, they knew of Tour fever and they were very much looking forward to welcoming the race to the Calder Valley. Sadly though her husband Tony died soon after, before he had a chance to see the riders visit his native Yorkshire.

That was a hard winter, but the human spirit is strong and come the spring, Julia was keen that Mytholmroyd bells should be a part of the festival.

So with the nucleus of the local ringers, myself and Derek and Ronalda (my festival saviours) we mustered a band.

We agreed on a plan for the day. An accompanying press release went out via the press agency and we did indeed attract visitors.

Meanwhile, the exact composition for this pioneering duet had now been finalised.

I don't know how familiar you are with sheet music – pages and pages of tiny notes scattered like ants across strange bars, in a manner which can look and sound quite beautiful, but yet be respectfully challenging to perform.

So too, bell-ringing methods can appear somewhat daunting as you saw in chapter 5.

Dave struck a nice balance in his little composition for us though.

'F E C D pause F E C D', he said. 'Ring out F E C D as a play on the central theme of the piano piece.'

Now, you are probably looking at that and thinking, come on, that's easy. And in a way it is. But remember this is bells.

It's okay playing four single notes on a piano. You just press the key, get your timing right and make sure you don't press any other keys.

With a bell, however, you are pulling a forty-foot rope with a half-ton shell of metal swinging full circle high above you and hopefully coming to rest on a fine balance after rotating 360 degrees.

It is not uncommon to pull too hard or too soft.

If you do so, the bell rotates again and it strikes again.

That's why you sometimes hear the bells strike thirteen or fourteen or more when being rung by hand at midnight to welcome the New Year in.

For us, 'F E C D pause F E C D' was just eight strikes on four bells, but if we failed to 'stand' any of the bells it would be as disrespectful and jarring as if Pavarotti had gone into hiphop mode at the end of that long note which concluded BBC Television's theme song for the 1990 FIFA World Cup in Italy.

But we had to be bold. This was not a challenge to be fazed by. We could do this.

In the end, we actually had a kind of remix. We had a discussion with Dave, on the day, up the tower. As he watched the actual manner in which the bells are rung, he decided an even better lead in to Kathryn would be 'F E C D pause F E C F', finishing on bottom F. In bell-ringing terms that was '1 2 4 3 pause 1 2 4 8.'

You can hear our actual performance on my website, in my summary of bell-ringing for Le Tour.

In the event we played a blinder. Just listen to those crowds cheering in the background at the start and end.

Hands up though, number three rang in the wrong place and I struck number eight three times. At least that was F though ...

Nevertheless, we had a whale of a time.

We welcomed a good many non-ringers to come and have a go on the bells. Hopefully, that may have led to the prospect of a new ringer or two.

There was a great craft fair in the church halls and at this point I should introduce Jane O'Neill of Abundant Glass. Jane has kindly shared one of her Tour de France artworks for the cover piece of this book. I'll let her tell her own story shortly. But she was one of the exhibitors at the fair. I had been struck for some time by her representation of cyclists in the Yorkshire scenery and her image of Cragg Vale has pride of place by the desk where I write this book.

And there was, of course, the piano.

To see the aerodynamic, rainproof windshield and the eighteen-bike PianoPorté in the flesh was quite amazing. To see the TV cameras around it was fascinating. And to run with it up the hill was an honour.

I couldn't run far, I had a Tower open day to help with still, but rest assured once I had finally 'set' that bottom F, I was running down the short spiral stairs in my polka dot shirt faster than Mark Cavendish exiting that underpass near the Place de la Concorde before winding up for the finish line on the Champs-Élysées. I made better progress up the Cragg on foot than I had in my car in the roadworks six months earlier.

'The Grand Departs' featured in *The One Show* on BBC1 that week.

The PianoPorté made a reappearance for the Festival in the Fantastical Cycle Parade in Todmorden three weeks later. Its biggest honour, however, would be to become the centrepiece of the Yorkshire section of the Lord Mayor's Parade in London later that year.

Eighteen bikes bolted together is a quite remarkable machine.

Eighteen bikes pulling a grand piano is something else.

We were honoured to play a small part in such an amazing event.

The PianoPorté meanwhile beat all expectations. They reached the summit in three hours fifty-two minutes, well ahead of schedule and even with a refreshments stop at The Robin Hood en route.

Three months later, on Sunday 6 July, the Tour de France riders did the climb in somewhat closer to seventeen minutes.

But they weren't pulling a grand piano.

CHAPTER 25

JUNE 2014 – CYCLE TO CHURCH SUNDAY AND THE GRAND DÉPARTY FOR MARIE CURIE

Outside of my Tour de France life I also enjoy cycling to work. I do, as you can see, have an incredibly diverse range of interests.

I am blessed with a scenic journey to Chesterfield, climbing though moorland out of Sheffield and touching on the edges of the Peak District. The landscape makes it an uplifting experience and the effort you put in more than pays back in terms of a healthier body and a positive mindset when you arrive at work. I am convinced that exercise leads to a more productive day.

2014, however, was probably my poorest year in a long time for cycling to work. With a heavy task-list for Le Tour, something was going to have to give if I was to keep the wheels on at home and at work. Ironically, it was the bike wheels that gave.

Nevertheless, I could always find time between midnight and 2 a.m. to plan another event for the Yorkshire Festival and, sure enough, another idea plopped out of my head.

Have you ever said 'I'm going to set a Guinness world record' for such and such? Go on, who hasn't said that at some point? Everyone wants to be a record holder.

So too, it transpired, do vicars, church congregations and vendors of industrial grade cling film. The cling film being important if, for example, you wanted to cover eighty square metres of carpet at the front of church in order to perform an official count and Pentecost blessing on a few hundred potentially oily or potentially wet bikes and their owners.

Yes, the idea was to go for a world record for the most people cycling to church for a Sunday service.

There were four things that led me to this idea:

1. To do something about declining church attendances – while millions of people happily sign up as Christians on the census, they are nowhere to be seen on Sunday. In church, we have a very valuable message and fellowship to share. Perhaps cycling could help reach the parts that the reading from the pulpit couldn't.

2. To support Marie Curie Cancer Care, the charity partner of Le Tour in Yorkshire. I'd been inspired by meeting the Marie Curie team in Harrogate at Y14. I'd been struggling with how to help them until now …

3. A response to the basic hunter gatherer instinct of 'I want to set a record,' and

4. It was a good excuse to get my bike out.

And so, without further ado I suggested to Gary, our vicar, that we could do a Tour de France-related event at our church, All Saints Ecclesall in Sheffield.

My basic sales pitch was not perhaps as sharply defined as it could have been, we were a couple of miles off the race route, the church calendar was already full and all the approaches to the church broadly involved ski slope or scree slope ascents and descents. It was great for a hill climb. It was not the stereotypical flat terrain that novice 'cycle to church' bike riders may gravitate towards.

Nevertheless, Gary saw the potential.

If this was *Dragons' Den*, then I had just secured my first investor. The thing was that next I needed 'investors of time' and that's something that is harder and harder to get these days. Life is very busy, work life balance is firmly tipped towards work through insidious devices like the Blackberry and committing to organising a mass participation event from scratch is just not something that you take on lightly.

I was already drowning in events though so I was okay. Another event could not sink me. I was fully submerged and running on adrenaline.

For a busy church office team though (or more precisely a busy church office individual, Helen) this was a leftfield idea for which we had no budget, no time and no photocopier paper. Cling film and other strategic enablers were far off the radar at this concept stage.

However, the vision was clear and Helen is an inspiration to anyone confronted by the proverbial camel needing pushing through the eye of a needle. She made it happen.

This was clearly the sort of fun event that would be good for church outreach, good for families and a great link with Le Tour and with a very good cause.

It would also turn out to be a fresh angle on Pentecost – the Lord filling his new church with the Holy Spirit and energising Jesus's disciples to share the word of God. With Cycle to Church Sunday we would energise the communities of south-west Sheffield and put a Tour de France spin on one of the pivotal sermons of the church year.

I now needed to crack on with some PR.

Being knee deep in the Yorkshire Festival already, as leader of the 'Bell-ringers Herald Cyclists' event, I thought it would be simple to launch 'Cycle to Church Sunday for Marie Curie' as a fringe event in the festival. I underestimated the challenge.

The issue, and rightly so, was that YFest was a festival of arts and culture, not a festival of faith and fundraising. In practice, YFest did embrace and celebrate a very broad spectrum of community groups, including faith groups, but it was clear that my new event needed a broader rationale.

We needed to ramp up the arts and culture aspects if it was to qualify for the fringe.

We weren't, at short notice, going to attempt to turn it into a music festival. Much as we were blessed with a wonderful depth of musical talent in Ecclesall, from recitals to rap, and from bass guitar to bagpipes, the last thing I needed was to try to organise a Glastonbury.

No, this would have to draw on the heritage of the building and its environment instead – its stained glass, its tombstones and the stories shared by the images and texts therein.

I don't know about you, but in addition to cyclists I follow the Sheffield General Cemetery Group on Facebook. That is a group of kind-hearted volunteers working to preserve and promote the architectural and social heritage of our graveyards. They care for places where the founding fathers of our city are buried and where their stories are the story of coal and iron and steel and the role played by Yorkshire as a powerhouse of the Industrial Revolution.

I discovered this group via Timewalk Project. They, in turn, are enthusiastic folk, whose story I will share in a few pages time, and who saw the potential for integrating Sheffield history into Stage Two of Le Tour de France 2014, 'The Steel Stage'.

What we found was that there was indeed keen interest in stained glass and graveyards. What Helen found in our church office was that we also had two very nice pamphlets already in place sharing photographs and narratives of the windows and the churchyard. Significantly, as First World War centenary commemorations approached, we also had some rare WW1 links.

Here's an extract from my festival event submission.

Event Name	Cycle to Church Grand Départy – spokes and steel and stained glass
Organisation	Ecclesall Parish Church
Artists	Local folk
Type of event	Community participation. Cycling, heritage, architecture, faith
Dates	Sunday 8 June
Audience	Local community, schools and children's organisations, those interested in Sheffield heritage
Brief event description	Ecclesall celebrates Le Tour de France with Cycle to Church Sunday, supporting Marie Curie Cancer Care. Explore Sheffield heritage with stories of the great steel founders buried here.
Full event description	Cycle to church and join us in our Grand Départy for Marie Curie Cancer Care on Sunday 8 June at All Saints Parish Church, Ecclesall.
	In the spirit of Le Tour, we have a cycling-themed service. We are trying to create a new record for the most bicycles ever ridden to a Church service. The most number of bicycles ever ridden to a single church service in Sheffield? Or Yorkshire? Or England? Perhaps even the world?

Full event description (continued)	In recognition of Stage Two of Le Tour, The Steel Stage, we also invite you to explore our churchyard and stained glass windows to find out more about the pioneers of the steel industry who are buried in this churchyard, one of the largest in Sheffield: steel founders such as Mappin, Wilson, Jessop, Jonas, Hadfield, Osborn, Tyzack and Brown. So too are 19 First World War soldiers including Sgt Arnold Loosemore, a rare Victoria Cross holder not awarded posthumously.
	The theme for this Cycle to Church service on Pentecost Sunday will be the 'wind of the spirit' and there will be a retiring collection for Marie Curie Cancer Care Fund – the first ever Tour de France charity partner.
	Imagine it – people from all over Sheffield cycling to All Saints to be part of our morning service for all ages. Everyone who cycles their bike to church that morning could help be helping us to create a new record; as well as helping Marie Curie Cancer Care.
	So please leave your car at home and cycle to church. We will need to make sure that we count all the bicycles accurately so you will need to arrive at All Saints with your bicycle by 10.30 a.m. at the latest.
	Please come to church that morning wearing your latest cycling kit. And invite your friends to ride along with you and bring some money for the collection. It's going to be a fantastic service and we want as many people as possible to fill the church and to create a new record.
	Happy Cycling … And don't let the wind in your tyres go flat.

And with that we were sorted. We had a cultural event in place.

In a way, looking back, that all sounds quite simple. Almost off the shelf.

In fact, it took ages. With all the other stuff too, I could write a trilogy about 2014. Maybe I will. Let's see how sales of this book go first. But as regards 'Cycle to Church Sunday' it was a big task.

Despite the existing pamphlets, I spent several happy hours scouring the churchyard and windows for photos for the website, and Helen spent goodness only knows how long on administration, correspondence and cling film to deliver it.

I had absolutely no idea how many people were going to turn up for our service; I had no idea what part the weather might play and I had little idea who in church cycled already let alone who else might pick up on our adverts.

It was with some trepidation that we set off from our house, a little bit late, a little bit tense, a little bit wobbly, for this next in a long line of 'Tour de France events' in the early summer of 2014.

When I saw we were six cyclists not just three, 100 yards from our house, a moment of optimism came to me. When it was a dozen by the top of the road I was happy we had smashed any previous record for Ecclesall.

But when I pushed round to the path on the north side of the church I was blown away. The bikes wove all the way round the church walls, up the path, through the lychgate, on to the pavement and down to the church halls. That was a good 300-yard queue. That was pleasing. And there were yellow shirts, green jerseys and polka dots in there too. #sorted #breatheagain.

We got two prominent articles in the *Sheffield Telegraph*. We got 209 people cycling on the day. And we raised £1,153 for Marie Curie. Our congregation of cyclists filled the churchyard in a front page photo shoot after the service.

Oh, we had bunting too. Our family spent the best part of a day cutting and stringing Marie Curie Tour de France bunting triangles. And, we had a drinks gazebo which didn't blow away.

We had an inspirational sermon about getting the breath of the Holy Spirit in your tyres. Sermons are recorded and made available as podcasts on our church website. I apologise in advance if, for reasons of space, some have been archived by the time you visit.

Now, to return to the original idea, we didn't get a world record.

The record proposal that I submitted to Guinness was as follows:

CLAIM TITLE – MOST BIKES IN A CHURCH SERVICE
Record details – inviting congregation, friends and community to join us to attempt the world record for the most bikes in a church service. This being the month before Le Tour de France comes to Yorkshire. It will be measured by the number of bikes inside the church building at the 11 a.m. service on Sunday 8 June 2014.

Their reply was:

> Dear Mr Rod Ismay,
> Thank you for your application to attempt a record you describe as 'Most bikes in a church service'.
>
> Currently, Guinness World Records cannot accept your proposal for this as a new record category.
>
> However, we have searched our Records Database and identified a different record, which may be well-suited to your record-breaking aims. We hope that you are interested in attempting this record category as an alternative to the category you proposed.
>
> This record is:
> 'Largest parade of motorcycles.'
> Please note that your application is now for breaking the record largest parade of motorcycles and you will have to meet all criteria in the attached guidelines to break this record. If you are not interested in breaking this record, please ignore this email.
> The current record to beat (current as at the date of this letter) is:
> although we do not currently list any 'official' record for the largest parade of motorcycles, you will no doubt be aware that there are many large motorcycling events and rides that claim to have in excess of 20,000 participants. Although not official, we would nonetheless regard this as the minimum acceptable benchmark for any inaugural record in this category (since, in our opinion, any ride of less than 20,000 would have little credibility within the motorcycling community anyway).

I was never able to reconcile this, I was never able to draft a quality counter-proposal and I never found enough motorbikes to make a credible bid for the idea they sent back to me.

We just had to carry on, secure in the knowledge that we were at least setting a cycling record for Ecclesall if not the world. Whatever the position regarding world champions, we were satisfied we had brought our community together in fun and in worship. Many seeds were laid whose stories will play out in due course and many friendships were made that can only happen when you challenge the norm and do something different.

What I do know, regarding attendance records though, is that the CTC (Cyclists' Touring Club) happened to have an annual cycling service at Coxwold in North Yorkshire during the Festival. I was unaware of this at the outset, but I spotted it in CTC communications later on, noting that they broke 300 with their attendance and so I emailed them after the event. It turns out that they have bell-ringing for their service too and they would welcome help from more ringers in future years. Ooh, I wish I'd known earlier. It was a fringe event in the festival too. Fabulous. Well done CTC The record may perhaps be yours. For now ...

Finally, for this chapter, and before I let Marie Curie and Timewalk Project say a word, I just need to mention a cyclist from t'other side of The Pennines. As I paced the queues of shiny and dusty bikes, my eyes were attracted to the sleekest of recumbent bikes. Who could this be? Where could the rider be from? It turned out that he was a Lancastrian in Yorkshire. Will had cycled a not inconsiderable distance to be with us from Cheshire, leaving at a refreshingly early hour and crossing the Pennines on the way. Even if our church didn't have a record, Will got one on the day – the longest journey to our service.

Many great things happened that day. We must do it again.

Donations to Marie Curie would continue to be most welcome and you can do so direct on their website.

A word from Marie Curie:

Marie Curie is the UK's leading charity for people with any terminal illness. The charity helps people living with a terminal illness and their families make the most of the time they have together by delivering expert hands-on care, emotional support, research and guidance.

Marie Curie employs more than 2,700 nurses, doctors and other healthcare professionals, and with its nine hospices around the UK, is the largest provider of hospice beds outside the NHS.

As well as this they support people throughout their illness by giving practical information, support from trained Helper volunteers and being there when someone wants to talk.

Marie Curie was honoured to be chosen as the charity partner of the Tour de France Grand Départ 2014 by Welcome to Yorkshire Chief Executive, Gary Verity. Gary is a patron of the charity and has been a fantastic supporter of the organisation, following the care given to his wife before she sadly passed away.

And a word from Timewalk Project:

I am grateful to Joyce Bullivant of Timewalk Project for her help and advice in transitioning our event from simply a cycle to church and into an opportunity to celebrate the heritage of our city.

In her words …

We started Timewalk project in November 2013, with the aim of promoting heritage in the city by mapping out what was there and publicising the hundred or so walking trails that were already out. After liaison with the cyclists of Sheffield Friday Night Ride we started listing cycle trails as well. Our aim was to have a one-stop place for people interested in Sheffield's heritage. That also meant listing all the events. There are around 2,000 a year.

When I heard there was a Le Tour presentation at the Town Hall I signed up for a ticket. I was quickly aware from the presentation that this was going to be much more than a lot of brightly clad cyclists whizzing past. The last cycle race I had watched as a bystander was the Milk Race many years ago. I have watched Le Tour on TV from time to time so I know the basic strategy etc, but the razzmatazz, well that's something different. They said they wanted bell-ringers and brass bands and as many community groups as possible.

The exciting thing was any group could join and I could see the potential for the heritage groups to get free advertising and raise some funds too. Wincobank was an obvious group because even before we knew the exact route it was clear that at very least helicopters would be going overhead. I started emailing every group I had contact details for and said to them this is the chance of a lifetime. My emails meant that groups were alerted two months before the Council got around to talking to them. Even then it was a very short timespan to get organised. Many thought they had to be on the route, so I emailed around again and even gave talks and said the only qualification you need is to be in Yorkshire.

The result was a lot of people and groups I knew joined in and we had one great party and at the end we crowded together to see the greatest cycle race on earth. I was where the stage winner broke away. He went on to win Le Tour overall, so it was a great moment. Le Tour showed Sheffield two things. They have a council who can mobilize to organize an international event in a matter of months without a hitch, and a great enthusiastic group of people who like cycling and having fun.

My greatest achievements were getting the Worrall Festival linked in, doubling the number of participants in the annual Yellow Duck Race for Friends of Porter Valley and getting Sheffield Cathedral the info early enough for them to make a successful bid to be part of the Yorkshire Festival. I also helped push through Twitter and Facebook for people to help the Friday Night Riders decorate Burngreave and Brightside.

My daughter tells me Cambridge asked why they couldn't have all the decorations we had in Yorkshire.

CHAPTER 26

TV UP THE TOWER – 'THE BIG RING' IS ANNOUNCED

'Hello Rod, my name's Martin Green, a producer working with Welcome to Yorkshire. I'd like to include church bell-ringing in the opening ceremony of Le Tour de France and I'm told you're the man to sort it. I wondered if you might be able to give me a call.'

It was Friday 13 June and there were now only twenty-two days until the Grand Départ.

That meant twenty days until the opening ceremony at the FD Arena in Leeds.

I'd bought my ticket a good few weeks earlier and was keenly looking forward to seeing the Tour teams on the stage. It was not far away now.

'Rod, this is embargoed, but would you be able to host an ITV *Calendar* film crew at a church one day next week, to film an interview which will be part of the formal announcement to the world of the 'Big Ring' for Le Tour de France in Yorkshire? Your idea of church bells is great. We'd like to make them part of the opening ceremony. We'd also like to invite the people of Yorkshire to join us by ringing their own bells wherever they are sometime between 8 and 9 p.m. during Gary Verity's welcome address at the ceremony. Can I put you in touch with Graham, who is handling the press links for me. He'll let you know exactly which day the announcement and filming need to be.'

It was at times like this that I got very excited … and just a little bit scared.

I wasn't doing much actual bell-ringing at the moment, I'd got an exceedingly demanding project on at work and I'd just agreed to find a church and a full band of ringers during the working week, potentially at a day's notice.

Ce sera une bonne journée de travail. This would be a good day's work. So long as I delivered.

Now I mentioned at the start of my story that I had some confidantes at work, people who kind of rode the journey with me, at our desks in Chesterfield, in the foreign fields of Derbyshire.

I also had some confidantes in the world of ringing. Jean, at Penistone St John's, was one of them.

Jean was secretary of the Barnsley & District Society of Change Ringers, she was a keen member of the band at Penistone and, at risk of narrative which could be misconstrued as age discriminatory, she was retired. That meant she had a thriving network of similarly retired bell-ringers who might just be able to accommodate a daytime TV session but one where you were actually on camera as opposed to shouting at a game show from the sofa.

Penistone, in turn, was one of my most favourite peals of bells in the whole of the country. I admit that I have only rung at 200 or 300 of the 5,000 or so towers in our land, but of those I was convinced that Penistone had the very sweetest sound.

I, therefore, rang Jean and told her the plan. And the secrecy of it.

Jean made a few calls and quickly confirmed to me that ringing for ITV at Penistone would be fine and that there was a good shortlist of ringers we could call on. The only thing was, 'They do have busy diaries (ringing, shopping, gardening, collecting pensions, I thought) so you'll need to give them plenty of notice.'

'Oh yes,' I said. 'At least a day's notice.'

We lived on the edge that summer.

It was the following Tuesday when Graham was able to confirm the announcement date.

'Rod, it's going to be tomorrow, 18 June. I'll give you the mobile for Chris, ITV's editor. If you give him a ring you can sort out the timings. Let me know how you get on.'

Like the day of my first Tour Roadshow, my diary that Tuesday said London. The previous year, for the Tour Roadshow, I had been able to rearrange my travel plans. This time, however, I was already in London and in a slightly heated meeting.

I discreetly texted Jean from under the table. I ensured my phone was on mute so as not to disrupt the flow of discussion of strategic imperatives. We agreed on the vision for cultural change on top of the table.

Under the table, I frantically exchanged texts with Jean to confirm a band and film crew for 2 p.m. the next day.

Win, win: meeting sorted and ringing sorted.

In the process, my smart phone, which I had taken out especially for Le Tour, began to reach its allowance for the first time.

Wednesday was pleasingly sunny.

I arrived a good half-hour early, having tipped off my mum (under strict embargo) that it might be a good day to pop into Penistone.

As I stood by the lychgate thinking about the filming to come, I suddenly remembered Cycle Penistone, the local group supporting cycle development and the Trans Pennine Trail. Wouldn't it be good to get them involved too?

I had, of course, by this time lost all sense of the politeness of giving people notice.

I ran to their offices, past the British Legion, past the former N.C.B. coal depot and past the asphalters ready to lay the next toppings of tarmac on the soon to be 'roads of France.'

'They're in a board meeting,' the bloke said in the bike hire shop downstairs.

'That's okay,' I said, 'This'll cheer them up. Can you get them down please?'

I admit it was a bit abrupt, not really like me, but down they came and in a matter of minutes so too did the Cycle Penistone road banners and the cheerleaders.

We now had a true 'bells and bikes' reception committee for ITV, and Cycle Penistone did indeed get an interview. Nice one.

The filming was kind of over in a flash. Simon, with the camera, was wonderfully understated as an interviewer. It was a friendly chat, man to man about the best thing in Yorkshire since sliced bread.

We posed for the camera and I asked the camera to pose for us. We each got our footage and Simon enjoyed the bells.

Filming in the ringing chamber was fun, filming the actual bells was a revelation to our TV crew and the clock mechanism on the intervening floor, with its bright brass wheels and pendulum and whirring, was a big attraction too.

With some relief I texted Graham to tell him it had all gone well.

'Great,' he said. 'Now can we have four more towers, one each night for the next week, plus one more for live coverage on the ceremony day itself.

We could have used Penistone but it's not on HD film so we need a wide screen format.'

The jobs were suddenly stacking up. This had been eighteen months' hard work cajoling the ringers of the county to be ready for race weekend and now, with a matter of days to spare, I needed to find five friendly towers who would take film crew and be up for possible live coverage on global TV.

Thankfully, I had a better idea now as to which tower correspondents were best at picking up telephone calls. It had been a painful process finding out, but a good network now kicked in.

I checked my Yorkshire Association of Change Ringers handbook to see which churches practised on which night of the week.

I looked for some variety in a sense of number of bells; six, eight, ten or more. I looked for variety of location in order that should there be outside shots, it would yield compelling images of our county. I also looked for a representative population of all ages of ringers.

With a whirlwind series of calls and a little gentle reassurance, I soon had the following itinerary for ITV.

Wednesday 25 June	Cawthorne, near Barnsley	6 bells
Friday 27 June	Chapel Allerton, Leeds	6 bells
Sunday 29 June	Ossett, near Wakefield	15 bells
Monday 30 June	Masham, in the Dales	10 bells

Chapel Allerton had featured on BBC Radio 4's *Bells on Sunday* just a few weeks earlier and were a bright set of bells, located just 100 yards or so from the route of Stage One of Le Tour. The riders would process past en route from the 'Départ Fictif' in Leeds City Centre to the Royal Party at the 'Départ Réel' at Harewood House. Their tower captain, Pete, had been a keen help to me throughout the campaign and I was delighted that they were able to host the film crew.

Cawthorne was not on the race route, but this was about involving the whole of the county. They had a young band and they were led by Brian, who had tried so hard to get me through that ringing at Bradfield months earlier. Like Jean, he too had been a constant voice of support throughout the project. This was a richly enjoyed evening for this beautiful little village and for a community which would go on to win a place on the route of Stage Three of the subsequent year's inaugural Tour de Yorkshire.

Ossett, again, was not on the race route, but it was the home of the hugely inspiring Woolly Bikes creator, Cassandra Kilbride, and it was hosting a practise by Yorkshire's championship winning youth band, The Tykes.

The Tykes and young bands like them are the future of the art of ringing. We need more of them. They enjoyed being on film.

Finally, there was Masham, representing North Yorkshire and the final miles of Stage One of Le Grand Départ weekend. Here was a beautiful tower and spire, an enthusiastic band, and a choice of breweries to end a busy week of filming.

Simon, the cameraman, learnt the basics of ringing in the process. Brian rarely lets a visitor up the tower without ensuring they have a go on the bells. He certainly wasn't going to let ITV escape.

I wish I could share some photos of the filming of these four towers, but the reality it seems was that our star struck ringers were so busy smiling for the camera that they had little chance to snap the action themselves. But, if you were in the Leeds FD Arena on Thursday 3 July then you saw them on the big screen, didn't you? They weren't bad, were they?

Over and above the four pre-recorded towers, I then engaged Leeds Minster to be the band for live coverage on the night. I was torn between Otley, whose story of a new band was just so wonderful, and the minster who were the twelve bells champions of our county.

The deciding factor was logistics. Leeds Minster was near the arena whereas Otley was a half-hour drive away. That sealed it. And so the ringers of Leeds Minster enjoyed an evening with BBC *Look North*.

I came up for air.

Just the race weekend to sort now.

Simples …

CHAPTER 27

ANOTHER BIKE IN THE WALL

By now, organising the church bell-ringing for Le Tour had dominated my life for eighteen months. In fact, a year later, as I write this, it still does. But that's my choice. Mrs Bellsandbikes has been very understanding.

However, there was more to Le Tour than just bells and bikes; a few other things had appealed to me in the build-up to the race. I mentioned some of the other Yorkshire Festival events in an earlier chapter. They were just great.

But there was something else that excited me along the race route. Not only were there churches and bells at every turn, but there were also dry stone walls. Hundreds of miles of dry stone walls.

Hoylandswaine has a goodly share of them too.

We go blackberrying in Hoylandswaine every year. 'Blackberrying' (for the benefit of the international urban readers of this book) is the art of picking nice juicy berries from bushes on walls in far flung fields, getting your hands and cheeks dyed black in the associate feeding frenzy and picking insects from your teeth if you are unfortunate enough to find a grub inside your bounty.

In my youth, I guess it marked the turning of the seasons and the start of each new school year.

We would cross the Hoylandswaine bypass (it's been there forty years now but it's still the bypass to purists), we would say hello to Mr Helliwell and off we would go foraging in the walls and hedgerows of the fields between Hoylandswaine and Silkstone Common.

It was probably on our September 2013 blackberrying trip that I met Gary Helliwell, stepping out of his dad's farmhouse, as we counted our berries and watched the hens clucking by the old cow troughs.

'I'm arranging church bells for the Tour de France you know,' I said. 'There's other people thinking about choirs for Le Tour, canals of Le Tour and traction engines of Le Tour. Do you think we could perhaps do something to celebrate the dry stone walls of Le Tour?'

I don't know what plans were already in hand in the dry stone walling associations of Yorkshire, but it turned out that Gary was the chairman of the South Yorkshire branch and his committee were very happy to explore ideas for good publicity.

It came as a bit of a surprise though, in early June 2014, when my mum said to me 'Gary's got something to show you. It's behind the farm … '

He wasn't in when we turned up.

He runs training classes on walling and was probably out teaching people, so we walked through the farmyard, stepped over the puddles, climbed up a little bank between the piles of stone and then we, especially me, gasped in awe.

'Dry stone Wall Bike.'

So skilful and yet so simple.

I tweeted my photo of the wall that evening and my phone buzzed all night. Despite my very best endeavours in promoting church bells on social media, it was Dry stone Wall Bike that became by far my most retweeted photo ever.

The bike went on to be a landmark near the finish line of Stage Two of Le Tour de France in Sheffield. It was a Yorkshire Festival fringe event in its own right.

By bizarre coincidence, Gary and his family now live in the same bungalow where I spent my childhood years. He looks out on the same fields where I played football in summer and went sledging in winter and, further, to the car park of the Lord Nelson pub where my dad first taught me to cycle without stabilisers. Gary's TV probably occupies the same corner of the lounge where our 1980s Granada Rentals Panasonic Colour Viewer lured me into a Tour de France addiction all those years ago.

Gary does lots of dry stone walling classes. Have a go. Visit the DSWA website. I'll let Ian, the South Yorkshire branch press officer, tell you more below.

But I have one other walling story to add as well, and for that one I will let Gordon Simpson, cyclist and waller, tell you his tale. I met Gordon through Twitter. I was ensnared by two fabulous walls he had built as a celebration of cycling. His walls in Otley and in Harrogate are just amazing. Read on and be delighted by his creations. I think they are great.

Thank you Gary, Ian and Gordon for all your work here and for kindly allowing me to share your stories in this book.

Who knows, perhaps we could do a combined dry stone walling and bell-ringing event in a churchyard on the race route of a future Tour de Yorkshire.

Do you know what? I think we should.

Here are their stories in their own words.

A TOUR IN DRYSTONE
South Yorkshire Dry Stone Walling Association & the Tour de France
by Ian Neville, Press Officer SYDSWA

The Dry Stone Walling Association of Great Britain (D.S.W.A.) was founded in 1968 with the aim of promoting better understanding of the traditional craft of dry stone walling and encouraging their repair and maintenance. Dry stone walling has been practised for over 3,500 years in the British Isles and in recent years has undergone a revival as the landscape and environmental value of walls built sustainably from local materials has been more widely appreciated. D.S.W.A. has a network of regional branches stretching from the Isle of Skye in Scotland down to south-west England which promote walling in their locality by undertaking charitable projects, training new wallers and running the L.A.N.T.R.A. approved Craftsman Certification Scheme.

The South Yorkshire Branch of D.S.W.A has around 50 members, ranging in ability from professional Master Craftsmen to enthusiastic amateurs who all share an enthusiasm for walls and walling. Monthly meetings are held throughout the year and members are active demonstrating or competing at local agricultural shows. Other recent projects have included the construction of dry stone jumps at the Frickley Park Horse Trials course, repairing an historic ha-ha around the perimeter of Wortley Hall and last year the construction of a freestanding dry stone wall with a bicycle motif near the finish line of a memorable Tour de France stage in Sheffield.

Early in 2014, S.Y.D.S.W.A. applied for a portion of the funding being made available by Arts Council England to support cultural events in the Yorkshire Festival staged in the run up to the Tour de France race. When our application was successful we set about designing a feature wall to commemorate the race and to showcase our craft. A design was drawn up and materials sourced so that a trial wall could be built from local sandstone, Staffordshire millstones and Welsh slate. Once we were satisfied, the wall was disassembled and transported stone by stone to the Don Valley Grass Bowl in Sheffield where it was rebuilt for the public to see on race day, 6 July. In conjunction with the feature wall we also staged a photographic exhibition of local walling and brought along a wall composed of lightweight blocks for children to have a go at dry walling for themselves.

After the event the bike wall was taken down, but has been rebuilt outside our main training site in Hoylandswaine, four miles west of Barnsley, South Yorkshire. If you'd like to view the bike wall it's incorporated into the perimeter wall of Green Top Farm beside the steep section of the A628 bypass. Further information on dry stone walling can be obtained from www.dswa.org.uk nationally and from www.southyorkshiredswa.org.uk more locally.

THE CYCLING WALLS OF RIPLEY AND OTLEY
By Gordon Simpson, professional Dry Stone Waller
The Ripley Monument

I have been a professional Dry Stone Waller for over 30 years, becoming one of the UK's top wallers. Also a keen cyclist and member of Harrogate Nova cycle club, it seemed fitting that something should be built to remind people of the Tour de France coming to Yorkshire, so I set about finding a suitable site. Ripley seemed best, just before the sprint into Harrogate. It is also adjacent to the Sustrans cycle track.

Landowner Sir Thomas Ingilby was keen for it to go ahead. A design had been going through my head for a few weeks and so construction started seven weeks before the start of the Tour, firstly sorting out thirty-five tons of rock and stone. We started on site three weeks before the tour came through and we finished at 10 p.m. the night before the race.

During construction, teams came past to recce the route, giving us various signs of approval as they rode through clouds of stone dust. Brian Robinson opened it for us which was fantastic; a cycling legend and very nice man.

The Otley wall was constructed at home over three weeks and taken in two parts at 4.30 a.m. on the Thursday morning before the Tour.

This monument was partly funded by Otley town's 'voice your choice' community scheme. The design had to fit in with Leeds Council's restraints (size, height and position) which made things tricky with construction, but it turned out okay.

This wall was opened by Otley town's Mayor. It is situated on the approach to Otley from Ilkley on the right-hand side of the road.

CHAPTER 28

RIDING THE ROUTE – ON THE ATTACK IN OUGHTIBRIDGE

It was a long time coming, but eventually I had to get on a bike and actually ride some of the Tour de France race route.

Looking back it's a bit hard to explain, but somehow it was incredibly hard in 2014 to find time either to ring bells or to ride bikes.

My previous plan to ride between post offices on the race route, raising money for BBC Children in Need, had probably been a bit over ambitious for a cold November day. That, of course, had morphed into something completely different with the #PudseyBikeRide, and I think that was for the best. Our Pudsey Ears-shaped route made a pretty iconic image on the Friday night appeal show.

In the subsequent months there was little opportunity to get on the bike. Partly due to the weather, but mainly due to event administration: calling churches, writing press releases, preparing for TV programmes and trying to get ringers focused on the events to come in July.

My chances to ride the route were, therefore, diminishing alarmingly when up popped an invite from Sharp Consultancy recruitment agency, the week before the opening ceremony.

I guess it wasn't totally out of the blue. We'd had a good few mountain bike rides for accountants over previous years. Book keeping and bike keeping, we do them both. We do them with eagerness and we enjoy great climbs and dramatic views in the Peak District along the way.

The proposal this time was road biking, making a loop towards the end of the York–Sheffield stage of Le Tour.

We would meet in Worrall, twenty-three and a half kilometres from the end of Stage Two. We would climb the Côte d'Oughtibridge (formerly known as Jawbone Hill), then go off route through Greno Woods and Green Moor to get up to the polka dot Bank View Café at Langsett. From there, we would cut over the reservoir dam to join the race route again above Midhopestones and then follow it home through Bradfield before finishing back at The Shoulder of Mutton in Worrall.

I was completely out of training.

To be honest I'd never really been *in* training. My cycle touring holidays had been two-week bursts of Alpine col bagging preceded by no cycling and three months of steelworks audits. My more recent cycle to work activity was satisfying but by no stretch of the imagination was it high performance racing, 14 m.p.h. was pretty much my goal.

It was from this robust base that I decided the Sharp's route in itself was not enough and I needed to add a few extra miles to get the very best from the evening.

I determined that I would cycle from home to Worrall via the Rivelin Valley and seek to make my first ever cycle descent and ascent of the locally infamous Hagg Hill on the way. I was, I guess, adding my own 'prologue stage' to the evening's formal Stage Two ride. Hagg Hill, however, had the potential to add my epitaph too.

Sheffield is known as the city of seven hills.

I'm not sure the word 'hills' actually does justice to some of the brutes that you encounter while riding round it, but then 'seven Alps' wouldn't be a fair description either.

In the Alps you encounter roads that rarely exceed a ten per cent gradient and which instead take a very long but very much more gradual route to zigzag their way through the mountains.

In Sheffield, and in the case of Hagg Hill specifically, the builders just did a straight line. If you plopped a funicular railway on to it, no one would bat an eyelid.

My route to Worrall would play along the edges of these seven hills. Well, actually, it would take me, like a rollercoaster, straight across the saw tooth series of valleys on the west side of the city.

Up and out of the Sheaf Valley, down Hangingwater Road into the Porter Valley, up and over Crosspool into the Rivelin Valley and then a final climb through Wisewood and Wadsley to look down into the Don Valley.

I was ready for a pint by the time I rode into the car park of The Shoulder.

My fellow riders, however, did not seem to be in quite the same place in terms of liquids.

I arrived on my heavy steel framed touring bike carrying panniers full of coats, spanners and Mr Kipling apple pies. They arrived in air-conditioned cars, unloading magnificent carbon monocoque frames and carefully adjusting water bottles full of the very best that high energy sports drinks had to offer.

These lean riders were no more likely to have a pint before the ride than they were to put panniers on for it.

I took a professional swig from my water bottle and accepted that the pint was a long way off yet. I needed to focus on the ride, not the ale.

The Shoulder of Mutton is close to the end of a very long and very fast descent from the Côte de Bradfield. Anyone starting from its car park is left with just a couple of hundred yards freewheel down to Worrall Road before the billiard table tarmac of Le Tour meets the rutted grey tarmac of everyday Sheffield. The rider then enjoys a sweeping left-hand turn under bunting and the chance to gaze in awe on 'Up-Cycle', the Worrall Wheel, an enormous and colourful sculpture of wheels marking the excitement with which this valley awaited Le Tour.

The rider can then savour another mile or so of urban descent to the valley floor where the swings and slides of the Oughtibridge Tour de France Fan Park invite a stretching of legs before a battle on a big climb.

It was there, despite my lack of training, that I decided I needed to make an attack.

One of my favourite, but sadly now tainted, memories of previous Tours was the day in the Pyrenees in 1996 when Bjarne Riis pulled into the middle of the road on the climb to Hautacam and allowed all his close challengers to ride past him on the inside. He stared each one of them in the eye. Perhaps they thought he was tiring. One by one he slipped back past them all, to the rear of the group, then, with a blistering acceleration he roared past them all, took the stage victory, and laid the foundation for winning that year's race as the first new name on the trophy after five years of domination by Miguel Indurain.

For my part, I adjusted my toe clips (I don't have fancy pedals), I checked my pannier was shut, and I slipped back a couple of riders as I tried, unsuccessfully, to drink from my water bottle without burping.

I then, as Paul Sherwen says in the commentary box, 'put the hammer down.'
I roared up the field.

One by one I dropped them. Fourth, third, second, first. I was alone. I was leading the field.

I was wearing polka dots, I was on the route of Le Tour on a 'Categorie 3' climb and I had just taken my steel-framed bike past all those fancy carbon machines.

They did warn me though.

'Ey up, Rod. What's tha' doin'?'

For a few seconds, maybe 100 metres, I was leader on the road. I was 'tête de la course'.

It wasn't a long break, but it was worth it. It was worth it to be able to enjoy the moment and it was worth it to be able to reminisce about it. But it hurt me for the rest of the evening and I soon slipped down from King of the Mountains into that other bold red guise on the road, the Lanterne Rouge, the backmarker of the race.

The team were kind to me though. They tried to pace me back to the front, they tried to give me a slipstream to recover in and they tried encouraging language like 'you could always take a short cut.'

In the early 1900s Tour riders did indeed take short cuts. The worst of the offenders would simply take a train and hope no one noticed. Grenoside, however, is on a steep hillside far from any train tracks, far even from Sheffield's heroically named SuperTram. I had to keep pedalling.

We rode through the magnificent green leaved tunnel of trees that is the deciduous rain forest canopy of Greno Woods. We sped on towards Wortley Top Forge, the oldest surviving water-powered heavy iron forge in the world, and then we took the killer climb up to Green Moor. A little way past the summit, at the turn to Penistone, I finally relented and accepted the short cut.

I gave up any hope of reaching the polka dot café at Langsett that evening, but in return I would gain the chance to ride the full climb of the Côte de Midhopestones. The rest of the group would miss that, as they would take an earlier right turn over the reservoir dam at Langsett.

The Côte de Midhopestones was a tough climb.

David was assigned to chaperone me, perhaps to call an ambulance if I needed one. He welcomed the chance to take on the Côte, but as I stopped to take photos of bunting, I sensed he thought I was not as focused on the ride as I should be.

The fact is I genuinely was focused on it. It was just that the richness of the community decorations was as much a part of Le Tour for me as was the actual cycling.

Harsh as the Côte de Midhopestones was, there would be more challenges to come though. The next one being a challenge for my brake blocks and wheel rims, more than for my legs. It was the descent to Ewden Beck.

Here we had one of the most severe hairpins Le Tour is ever likely to encounter. This was the beautiful but infamous Strines Road where Ewden Beck presents a 180-degree hairpin on a 25-degree gradient, supplemented by adverse camber and a moorland spring washing over the exit from the corner.

Strines road began as a toll road for horse-drawn coaches. On rainy days, it had taken its toll on riders in the Tour of Britain, with some famous names including world champion Tom Boonen ending up in the undergrowth. Sunshine on Sunday 6 July must have been a massive relief to the riders in Le Tour and perhaps even more so to the truck drivers of the Tour publicity caravan, as rain would have made this corner truly treacherous.

The Beck is followed by another sharp climb, not long but very steep.

Magnificent views of the Peak District then begin to open up and the rider joins the long, exposed roads into and out of High Bradfield.

By this time, the accountants' peloton had come together again and I was in better shape. I broke away one last time, gaining enough gap to jump into the bracken and bilberry bushes, in order to get a ground level photo of our team as they raced into Bradfield.

Another ten minutes and we were back in the car park of The Shoulder, with a pint on the horizon.

Thanks Chris and Julian at Sharps for such a great ride. I'd recommend it to you too dear reader. The climbs, the views, the Tour tarmac and the fine food at The Shoulder of Mutton. Very, very nice.

They even had bunting up in the bar.

There was one more challenge for me though.

Hagg Hill.

The descent had been a little unnerving earlier that day. The hill is very steep and it was somewhat accentuated on that warm summer evening by the broken wall and tow truck tyre marks where a car had bailed out on the right rather than risk its brakes on the downslope.

At 11 p.m. fortified by my substantial meal, I prepared for my first ever ascent.

Given my foolish breakaway earlier, and the ballast from tea, the odds should have been against me, but my tyres held the gravel on the entry to the climb. I completed the steep first section and the responsibility of the polka dot shirt gave me that same cloak of invincibility as it had at the Tour roadshows the previous summer.

Yard by yard, metre by metre, I crawled up the hill.

The further I got, the more my legs burned and my chest pounded, but so too my sense of destiny became clearer and clearer.

The gravel passed, the entrance to the allotments eased by, the final ramp reared up and I was there, Hagg Hill turned right on to Bole Hill Road and the monster was tamed.

However, Hagg Hill is a little bit like the world famous Tour climb of Alpe d'Huez. Everyone talks about the twenty-one hairpins of the Alpe and they all see the sprint in the ski resort as the finish, but the reality for a purist climber is that the true finish (the summit) at 1,999 metres above sea level is the Col de Sarenne, a further nine kilometres beyond the town and 133 metres higher than the Tour stage finish line.

Hagg Hill, by comparison leads on to Bole Hill Road, then Back Lane and finally Stephen Hill, all relentlessly climbing to the final summit near the Sportsman inn at Crosspool.

I've climbed Alpe d'Huez on a steel frame, with a pannier, and then carried on to bag the Col de Sarenne. Stephen Hill had, therefore, to be conquered.

And it duly was.

The bunting at the allotment shops just before the final bend was a fitting backdrop to the day.

For my sole ride of the Tour route in the year of Le Tour Yorkshire, this was a very satisfying evening.

CHAPTER 29

THURSDAY 3 JULY –
'THE BIG RING' AND THE OPENING CEREMONY

It had been a rush, but also a delight, to organise filming at all those churches for the opening ceremony. I was now very much looking forward to seeing the products on the big screen.

As I thought about the weekend ahead though, it was probably too late now to have any more influence on the ringing for the Grand Départ. The weekend would simply be what it would be. For several churches, I still had no news. Would they ring? Wouldn't they ring? I was on tenterhooks.

Two more requests then came forward.

Firstly, to get as many churches as possible ringing on the evening of the opening ceremony and, secondly, to find another tower where the official film crew for the Yorkshire Festival could get footage of 'Bell-ringers Herald Cyclists' for the wrap up film of the festival.

For the opening ceremony, I had to email and hope. Yes I tweeted, yes I facebooked, yes I blew my phone allowance and yes Welcome to Yorkshire put out a great press release, but ultimately I had to hope.

Martin Green explicitly asked me the question 'how many towers and how many ringers will it be?' Little did I know that the answer would be cast in stone in Gary Verity's address to the world media at the ceremony.

I counted how many churches already had practise nights on a Thursday, I took a guess at how many more might join in and I said sixty churches. Then, with typically six to eight bells up a tower plus a few spare pairs of hands, I guessed we might average ten ringers in each tower.

Sixty churches and 600 bell-ringers went into the script.

With much joy, the final tally came in at over seventy. Phew!

For the Yorkshire Festival film, I turned to Sheffield's Anglican cathedral, St Peter and St Paul.

Here was a friendly band, with ringers who worked nearby and it was the venue for two festival events that week. Outside the cathedral, the 'Sheffield Festival of Colour, Space and Light' was taking people on a journey of music, dance and digital art in a walk-in inflatable art installation filled with vivid, striking colours made by natural sunlight. Meanwhile, in the cooler and calmer interior of the cathedral, the ten knitted woolly bikes had all come together for their formal showcase presentation to the world.

Our ringing would be a tribute to these festival events, a warm-up for the opening ceremony and a rich soundtrack for the festival film. I am indebted to Simon Reading for arranging a band at very short notice to make it all possible.

And so at 8 a.m. on Thursday 3 July, I dropped our son Thomas at his 'before school club', I vainly tried to do a couple of hours' work and I eventually jacked it in to make my way by bus to the cathedral.

My stalwart festival colleagues Derek and Ronalda came to help ring and we passed a very happy hour filming the woolly bikes before climbing the tower.

In the meantime, Natalie kindly let me get a selfie in the Welcome to Yorkshire race car and we chatted with David Lascelles, Earl of Harewood, reflecting on the overall success of the Festival which he had championed and chaired.

Our ringing went well, but you always need a 'take two' and a 'take three'. The biggest thing, in fact, turned out to be Alex, our cameraman's, fascination with the spiral stairs.

He was using a special gyroscopically stabilised camera, which hung in a frame, maintaining its balance regardless of the movement of its holder. It would create a special flowing effect to the film, but it was tricky, to say the least, to carry on a tight spiral staircase.

The finished product was great on screen. You can see it for yourself in 'Festival Rising' if you google the 2014 Yorkshire Festival. You can also hear the theme of bells running through the backing tracks.

I chatted to Lee, Alex's brother after the filming. I shared my experiences of the build-up to the race, I shared my hopes and joys and frustrations. We joked. He then announced 'Great, that's the interview done. I don't like to tell people that I am recording them on tape. It's better that way.'

I hope I was respectful. I think I was. I haven't had any complaints yet about anything I said. Yet ...

And with that, my work for the 2014 festival was largely complete. Except for getting to the opening ceremony followed by the small matter of the actual ringing for the race.

I was beginning to get a bit anxious about the time. Alex and Lee had kindly said I could travel with them to Leeds, but they had a bit more filming to do first and there were increasing reports of jams on the M1. They didn't seem to have a police escort so I opted for the train. I ran to the station in record time and once more I was the only passenger in red polka dots as the two-carriage train bumped and jolted its way through Elsecar, Wombwell and Barnsley.

Somehow, at the other end of the line I amazingly had a couple of hours to spare before the ceremony so I checked my street map, I wiped my camera lenses and I strode on to the race route of Le Tour.

Now the thing about my whole experience of the 2014 Tour (and the following year's inaugural Tour de Yorkshire) was that I spent more time on roadside decorations and music than I did on actual cycling. In Leeds, that day, I would at last get to see the real teams of Le Tour, but I had a couple of hours beforehand to further indulge my interest in street furniture and bunting.

Leeds, however, had gone a step beyond what I had become accustomed to. There, yellow bikes and bunting were overtaken by telephone boxes with Tour maps on, bike parking racks shaped like cars and polka-dotted bins. This was just up my street. Time flashed by as I photographed and tweeted my way around the city centre.

It was teatime when I took my seat in the Leeds Arena. A busy day of bell-ringing, knitted bikes and bins had passed happily. Now I was in seat 7, row K, block 108, as close as I could get to the stage, eagerly looking for celebrities and waiting with bated breath to see the bells on the screen.

The ITV *Calendar* team ran a warm-up from 5.30 p.m. before the main event started at 6.30. The voice of Le Tour, Monsieur Sebastian Piquet, then stepped on stage accompanied by UK sports commentary heroine, Jill Douglas, in a splendid and subtly polka-dotted number.

Seb is 100 per cent French but with the most perfect English and the most fluid transition from French to English. I yearn to have such linguistic skill and that ease of transition. Forget the cycling, this was a joy of oratory. Mrs Bellsandbikes later reported that he ticked the box for the TV viewer too. Zut alors, le competition!

What we then had was a kind of four-part show, while I carefully tried to balance a pint on my knee in one of those fragile plastic beer pot things.

Festival acts gave stirring performances at the ceremony. Hope & Social, who had involved so many communities in song in the build-up to the race led the way. Their Tour of Infinite Possibility had been a huge success and who knows what future singers and musicians may be inspired to come forward after finding their voice during that tour. They were joined by Opera North and by the spectacular bicycle dance routines of the Ghost Peloton riders clad in their LED light suits.

Films of the race route ran on screen, interspersed with soundbites from local communities sharing their crafts and welcoming the world to our county with a big bold 'Bienvenue à Yorkshire.'

The teams of world cycling processed across the stage, being interviewed by Jill and Seb. Mark Cavendish and Chris Froome predictably took the biggest cheers, but other heroes of the peloton, perhaps less well-known to non-cycling bell-ringers, captivated the crowd. Marcel Kittel and Peter Sagan certainly seized the moment.

The music of the evening ramped up with Alistair Griffin and Kimberley Walsh dueting on 'The Road', the anthem of Le Tour Yorkshire and the evening concluded with a cracking gig by Embrace.

But the pinnacle for a bell-ringer in block 108 was the welcome addresses of Gary Verity, for Yorkshire, and Christian Prudhomme for Le Tour.

Christian showed his new found and intense love for Yorkshire. His interview with Harry Gration two days later capped it all, 'The Tour de France is very, very popular but what we saw yesterday and today was unbelievable, incredible, amazing, astonishing!'

Gary then proceeded to take the ovation of all ovations. He was our sporting personality of the year, our ambassador for uniting nations, our master of the universe. The applause was long and loud. It was his vision and his passion that had led us to this climactic evening.

And in the middle of his speech came the bells.

'My greatest thanks for tonight is reserved for every man, woman and child who supported, encouraged and believed in our dream. As I speak, 600 bell-ringers across sixty churches across the county are ringing hundreds of bells in celebration of this moment, in itself an inspirational example of what we can achieve together. I am certain that thousands of young people across the UK will be inspired by the champions of cycling this weekend. This is our destiny – you are part of history – vive la Yorkshire vive Le Tour de France!'

I kid thee not, but I do believe that church bells got as much airtime as Cav in the opening ceremony. Now, although I could be perceived as being a bit biased towards bells, I am a big fan of Cav, but you should have heard the cheers as Gary looked to the screen and the ringers of Chapel Allerton, Cawthorne, Ossett and Masham did their stuff.

Brad, you did us proud with that bell at the Olympics.

But look how many bells we got into the Tour de France opening ceremony. Just look. We shifted more metal, in total, than that world record-setting, massive and iconic bell at London 2012. And we dominated the script.

Outside, the bells rang out across the county; mediaeval heavy metal. Serious weight moved in the towers and a big weight lifted from my mind; the bell-ringers of Yorkshire came good.

Gary, we thank you so much for the story you allowed us to play a part in. This was a very, very good ceremony. It would be hard to top that, but two more things happened before my very late arrival home after another polka-dotted train trip through Barnsley.

One thing was that I gate-crashed Sharon and Vernon's 'bunting champion' meal after the opening ceremony. Sorry! It was very kind of you to share some tapas with me. Sharon had just secured the world record length bunting title, Vernon was King of Cragg Vale and I was one very relieved bell-ringer. I knew they were in town and much as I would have liked tapas with Team Sky, there was a need for a bells and bunting celebration. We'd done it. Cheers!

But on the way to the tapas bar, I saw some mustard coloured trousers crossing the road. The trousers weren't alone. They were firmly wrapped around some sturdy legs and mustard could only mean one thing. No one else wears mustard. This was the Welcome to Yorkshire team.

I recognised Peter Dodd, commercial director, so I ran after them to congratulate them. And then I saw none other than Monsieur Bernard Hinault. Here was a five times Tour de France winner, wearing mustard trousers, walking towards Leeds railway station with a group who may, I suspect, have had a very refreshing pint first.

'Er, excuse me Peter. Well done! A cracking evening. I'm Bells and Bikes.'

'Yes I know. Thanks. Well done to you too.'

Now, we'd been in the same room at the Tour Roadshow in Sheffield but we'd not actually spoken directly before. But he knew me. Was I some kind of pin-up at Welcome to Yorkshire's offices? Who knows? But to get to the point.

'Would Bernard mind me taking his photo? What do you think?'

'Of course not. Look, give me your camera. Oy, Bernard. Arretez! Stop!'

And there I was, standing with Bernard Hinault, fumbling for my Yorkshire Festival flag and having my photo taken with a five-time Tour winner.

I jabbered some incomprehensible but very respectful French about the fabulous evening 'Je sonne les cloches. Il y a beaucoup d'eglises pres du route du Tour. C'est moi qui organise les sonneurs des cloches.'

'Magnifique!' he said, or something like that. We shook hands and he was gone.

I tweeted our photo and weeks later I found Bernard on Twitter. It was probably August or September when he joined the twitterverse. I tweeted the photo again, this time directing it to him. And then, I know not how, his Twitter profile changed to look strangely like that photo taken on my Blackberry. I zoomed in on it and there was a tiny bit of spotty polka dot sleeve to the right of him. My sleeve. Bernard Hinault was using a photo from my Blackberry for his social media profile.

Thank you Peter Dodd. I owe you one.

Next up, the race.

CHAPTER 30

SATURDAY 5 JULY – HARROGATE – THE GRAND DÉPART AND THE WRONG SIDE OF THE ROAD

For the race weekend we stayed in the Premier Inn near York railway station. The Premier Inn had much in its favour. If you were a fan of the Team Europcar cycle squad, it was handily located near the local Europcar rentals depot. If you were more interested in a great choice of pillows as advertised on TV, then they were all on demand, without the upset of Lenny Henry appearing on your bed. And if you wanted to ring the bells at St Martin's Coney Street, the hotel was on the same side of the road for easy access on race day. They don't talk about all these things on the hotel website, but they were important considerations for me. As well as the fact that Harrogate had not a room to spare.

And so we arrived in York on Friday evening on the 7 p.m. train; Sally, Thomas and I. We then met Peter and Anna, our teammates for the weekend. Peter and I had been best men for each other and we had enjoyed several cycling holidays in France, Italy, Spain, Ireland and Norway. We had cycled through Pyrenean snow together and in years gone by had regularly assembled bikes in airport waiting areas in happier times for air travel. We'd even conquered the giant Stelvio Pass in Italy with full panniers and a minor hangover from Barolo and pizza in Bormio. We were more than a match for planning and watching a bike race. We were also experienced in assembling and drying soaked tents in hotel rooms on cycle tours. The Premier Inn would no doubt be relieved to know that we had no wet tents in our luggage that Friday.

We did, however, have several cameras and we put them to full use that evening as we stared in wonderment at the fabulous window displays of the shops in York, with their cycle-themed welcomes for the race. Thirty minutes' free Wi-Fi rounded the evening off and before we knew it, the sun was rising, the bacon was frying and a cacophony of bedside alarms rang their little chimes as a foretaste of the clangour of bells and bikes that was to follow.

It was mid-morning when we arrived in Harrogate for Stage One. The train had a few spare seats when we left York, it was standing room only as we passed the densely packed and ironically named Cattal station and there were a couple of stops where it was like the worst rush hour tube train you have ever seen. The crowds kept rolling in but thumbs up to the brilliant staff of Northern Rail, standing helpful and firm, like human lighthouses, as the tide of humanity washed around them.

On my previous trips to Harrogate I had had to ask for directions. This time there was no such need, as we were pulled along by the river of people flowing inexorably in one direction only, straight towards St Peter's church.

Well, in fairness, they were probably going towards the Tour fan park and stadium zone all along The Stray, but The Stray is happily located within earshot of St Peter's bells so it was all the same in my book.

We followed the crowd, we could have surfed on it, Glastonbury, eat your heart out.

I hesitated when we hit The Stray though. There was one simple question, where to pitch up for the day to wait for the riders? The Stray was a long road and the options were varied and tempting. Spaces by the France TV cameras? A party with the Manxmen and their Cav flags? A picnic in the park? Or the shade of the bus stop just along from Betty's Tea Rooms.

Eventually we chose the latter. It was festooned with fine bunting, it had a perfect view of the big screen and it was facing St Peter's.

We fought our way across the pedestrian crossing. It probably took twenty minutes to make the whole journey from a funnel of fans on one side to a mêlée outside Betty's on the other.

Shortly afterwards the road crossing closed. Charity cyclists, children's groups and the freaky Festina watchman took over the road and as we cheered them on I realised I had a bit of an issue, we were stranded on the wrong side of the road for bell-ringing. It was a great view of the church tower but it was going to be a bit hard to explain to the local ringers who were waiting for me. Then the mobile networks became overloaded and went down, so I had no need to explain. I simply couldn't get a message to them if I had wanted to.

I did try to wave to them whenever they appeared on the tower top. I could hear the bells but I was just too far away and they could not hear or see me, no matter how bright my spotty shirt was. I was unable to phone them despite the fact I was standing next to a media village covering a square kilometre and packed with more satellite dishes and communications equipment than Jodrell Bank. In fact, distant galaxies will continue to hear echoes of this day for light years to come, but I couldn't get a text message across the road.

I have subsequently tried to apologise to St Peter's ringers. I truly was sorry, I had, after all, been preparing for this day for eighteen months. But sadly my text of apology soon afterwards was too little too late. I compounded the problem by referring to them as Harrogate St Wilfrid's instead of Harrogate St Peter's in a magazine article the next week. Truly, truly I ask their forgiveness and let me assure the readers of this book that St Peter's did a cracking job ringing for the race that afternoon.

I regret not being able to ring that day, but putting the bells on one side we had a great day by the bus shelter.

There was a real camaraderie in the crowd. It was probably like the banter on the terraces at football, but the difference was that we didn't have a reserved seat next to the same family who occupy the same row every Saturday. Here we were amongst total strangers and yet we were amongst friends. That's the thing about crowds at a bike race, you are always amongst friends.

The onion seller was a big hit and I made sure to get a photo with him. The lady in yellow shoes who insisted on taking up more pavement space than any other person in the whole of Harrogate by stretching her legs out for four hours was a focus of attention too, for muttering and staring at, not for backslapping though. Ned Boulting of ITV Cycling was a hit too. He came within six feet of me, I shouted loudly to him, but he didn't hear. And Thomas, who by this time was sitting on the barricades right under Ned's nose flatly refused to listen to my appeals to say 'Bonjour Ned.' I think, in fairness, Thomas had had enough of media coverage of bells and bikes by then. He just wanted to see the race.

As the afternoon began, there was a minor disturbance as a drunk bloke sat on a tree branch hanging over the crowd. It was funny at first but it gradually became life-threatening for him and for the reluctant crowd trapped below him. He eventually climbed down to a barrage of boos and hisses.

The happier roars though were for the awesome scenes on the big screen. We looked on in wonderment as the riders were greeted by William, Kate and Harry, the Royal send-off party at Harewood House. As they cut the tape and as the Red Arrows roared above them, we knew we were truly at the heart of the biggest event ever in Yorkshire.

The scenery was dramatic as the race made its five-hour journey across the county and we stood to attention the whole way. Fine images with mystical subtitles rolled over the screen: L'eglise de Holy Trinity Skipton, Le Chateau de Middleham, Le Côte de Grinton ... Yorkshire was the new France.

Our sliced ham and salmon held up well in the heat. Sandwich making when you can scarcely move your arms in the crush was a challenge, but it was all part of the experience. The chocolate was a bad idea though.

Replete from lunch, we then agreed to initiate some solo scouting missions to explore the neighbouring area while the main body of our team held our position by the road. Peter, Anna and Sally did not go far. I, however, was determined to check out the media village. As it happened, my Bells and Bikes business card did not carry sufficient weight to get me in, but I was at least able to visit the fabulous yellow mushroom porta-urinals of Le Tour that Ned Boulting had written about so vividly in his best-selling analysis of the race *How I Won The Yellow Jumper*. Getting back to our sardine-tin space by the road was a challenge, but it was worth it for the sights of the team coaches and the crowds in the fan park.

The backmarkers in the charity rides came in and Festina Man continued to hold the road and gradually the race approached with its strange and spectacular entourage of publicity vehicles. There were motorised Fruit Shoot lorries, chariots of McCain Oven Chips and, of course, no Tour being complete without it, the Happy World of Haribo. There was also a French optician chain and, although we may not recognise them on our own high street yet, their presence may have been for due diligence and market analysis ahead of some future venture-capital-funded Norman conquest.

It was the Yorkshire Tea lorry that got the biggest cheers though.

The moorland scene on the back of their truck was like a Skype connection to the race in the Dales as the lorries rolled up The Stray. The packets of Yorkshire Thé that they distributed were a touch of genius.

And then came the race.

Its outcome is well-documented.

There was a clash of wheels, Cav fell and a nation gasped in shock. The TV cameras zoomed in on David Cameron as he clasped his head in angst. The prime minister's body language spoke for the whole of the country.

Marcel Kittel took the stage and a million people moved on in disbelief. Marcel is a truly great rider and he is much loved in this country, but we had all waited eighteen months for Cav to win in his mum's hometown. This was a bitter pill to take. It had been a magnificent day but there was just a tinge of sadness.

But hey, take a look back at those images of the race: the crowds on Buttertubs, the Red Arrows, the royal guests, the wall of non-stop noise for 190kms. This was indeed the grandest Grand Départ.

This was also Yorkshire. We take our knocks and we get up again. Thus, as the fans set off to stake out their positions for Sunday and as the lorries moved in to take the barricades away, we donned our official merchandise caps, puffed out our chests and recharged our cameras full of megabytes of the most exciting scenes ever in this county.

Gary Verity and Christian Prudhomme were walking up towards Betty's as we made our way to Jakes restaurant for tea.

'Well done Gary, what a brilliant day,' I said as we passed. I didn't linger. I could see that they, like the nation, were in that mixed up state of excitement and yet shock at the surprise of the crash at the end. They, like us, needed a moment to absorb the enormity of the day.

We all moved on. We had another huge day to prepare for.

But hark! Who was that. Who could I hear rattling towards us festooned in yellow bike necklaces and carrying more cameras than a TV crew? It was none other than my ringing stalwarts, Derek and Ronalda. As the sun set on Stage One of Le Tour, our renegade bell-ringing PR machine reconvened in the upper room of a restaurant off The Stray and delighted ourselves with tales of a successful day.

They had defied all the doom-mongers about public transport and, with a happy marriage of bus and train, were able to savour the atmosphere in Wharfedale and in Harrogate on the Saturday. The next day they would do it all again too, ringing for the race in Silsden before getting a train to Meadowhall in order to see the riders on the infamous climb of the Côte de Wincobank, looking down on the domes of the shopping centre and towards the double decker motorway bridge that is Tinsley Viaduct. These were the juxtaposing backdrops to the most beautiful race in the world and these were the people whose passion made it the community success that it was.

We downed our pints and we joined the jolly conga snaking its way back and forth, back and forth, from the railway station, through the bus station and far, far beyond. A happy crowd gradually made its way back to York.

CHAPTER 31

SUNDAY 6 JULY – YORK – ROOFTOP TALES

Sunday announced itself to the world with complete indifference. It was like a wet November morning in a London hotel on a business trip.

On the inside we had a cross between *Fawlty Towers* and the Tower of Babel as voices of all nations competed for attention at the hot food counter by the gently crisping sausages.

On the outside, through the rising mist from the poached eggs, we saw a steady stream of hunched figures in cagoules, wandering slowly but purposefully like city dwellers on the quest for fresh milk while trying to send a text message.

In and amongst the cagoules we saw bikes too. Gradually, their numbers rose, the rain receded and the shiny wet waterproofs began to be overtaken by happy hi-vis Lycra. Slowly, very slowly, Sunday began to live up to its name.

It had been a late night that laid the foundation for this drizzly morning. Despite our endurance race, standing roadside for six hours the day before, I had been unable to resist a late-night photo session in York city centre afterwards, capturing more nocturnal images of churches, cobbles and Tour-themed windows. Thirty minutes' tweeting on the hotel toilet, lights on and extractor fan buzzing was, however, a bit unfair to have inflicted on Sally and Thomas on my return. It was certainly one way to use the free Wi-Fi allowance but, yes, it could have been better timed.

And so, as the sun gradually battled to reassert itself on the Grand Départ, we packed our bags and did a high-tech hokey cokey of smartphones and hairdryers on the hotel room plug to get ourselves in shape for the day ahead.

Our walk to the race was not long in distance, but it was slow in delivery. There were more shop windows calling out to my camera, there were other visitors to give vague directions to and there was a photo shoot on Bridge Street. Thomas was delighted to pose for a freelance photographer, waving a 'Go Froomey' sign. A couple of kindly Tour Makers were delighted to pose for our camera too.

Finally, we reached the junction with Spurrier Gate which led on to Coney Street, where we would join the bell-ringers a little later.

We secured a good position on the corner and joined in the happy banter of the crowd. There were cheers for all the pedestrians safely crossing the road, there was sympathy for a poor shop worker on tenterhooks about getting over at the last minute and there were roars of approval for some lady cycle commuter who seemed to have become stranded on the race route, oblivious to the barricades and crowds and ignorant of the motorcycle sirens getting louder and louder behind her on the road up from York race course.

I found refreshments at the aptly named Bells of York coffee shop and we were soon shouting loudly to those fabulous vehicles of the publicity caravan that had so delighted us the day before as well. Whether it was the Sheffield Hallam University Land Rovers, Yorkshire Tea or the Econo Bic pen van, our cheers were undiminished.

As the caravan continued, I left our family team to cheer the cyclists and I made my way to the bells.

St Martin's is an ancient building, respectfully restored after severe bomb damage in the Second World War and renowned for its large clock overhanging the main shopping street of York.

Outside, the ringers had placed a large advert encouraging people to come in and have a go. Inside, they hosted a great long table bedecked with cakes of all kinds. I asked for Tanya and Neil. I'd been corresponding with them for months but we'd not yet met. It was great to do so at last.

Their plan for the ringing was an exciting one. The bells would ring for the race, but we would also get to see the riders ourselves. They would facilitate this by setting the mechanism going which strikes the bells with hammers for pre-defined tunes. In the meantime we, the ringers, made our way across the roof to a vantage point looking both ways along Coney Street. The riders would pass directly below us and the helicopters, if we were lucky or colourful enough, might zoom in on us. Whether they did or not, I don't know. I think York Minster trumped us with a massive yellow square saying 'Allez Alleluia' on the roof of their central tower.

Nevertheless, the St Martin's ringers spread a big banner on their roof and I spread myself in polka dots next to it. You can but try.

It was a genuinely emotional time as the Lancaster Bomber did its flypast and as the low throb of the helicopters signalled the approach of the bikes.

With this signal, we rushed to the parapet looking down on to the street. Camera in one hand and smartphone in the other, I filmed the peloton pass by and I tried to take a snap of each supporting team car. Somewhere on the way Gary and Christian passed by again, greeting the fans from the Skoda lead car.

And then they were gone.

After eighteen months of preparation the job was done. Well sort of. I mean it eventually led on to the idea of writing a book, but in the sense of welcoming the riders, the job was done. Except that it wasn't. There were a dozen more churches along the race route yet to ring and what good work they did when their time came. For us in York, however, the remaining task was the crowd. We had a captive audience needing a new pastime for the day, and fortunately we had just the thing for them …

'Ici, ici, venez ici. Bienvenue à York. Bienvenue à bell-ringing. Ici. Le bell-ringing. Le belle ringeeeeng. Voulez-vous essayez le bell-ringeeeeng pour Le Tour de France. Poursuivez-moi. Joignons-nous. Nous vous souhaitez. Venez ici at allez la bàs. Le belle ringeeeeeng pour Le Tour.'

In hindsight people may have thought I was mad. Je ne sais pas. Whatever the case, I was in my element. Ringing a bell on the Android app on my phone and pacing Coney Street, shouting in Franglais to the international audience, I extolled the virtues of bell-ringing.

I'll not take credit for the throngs of people who did indeed come and have a go. There was a constant stream all afternoon and it was all credit to the good advertising of the local band, to the warm welcome they gave visitors and perhaps, I guess, to the quality of the cakes too. If my Franglais town crying also proved helpful, I would be delighted to know.

And with that, we took on a new member into our team, Jane, who had come down from Newcastle for the day. She had been to Reeth the day before to see Stage One and she was ecstatic about the atmosphere surrounding the race in the Dales. Thomas's godmother, she was now here to share our day in York and to enjoy a glass of wine or two over pizza.

Our day in York concluded with fine food, with a relaxing time in the shade of the trees listening to the automated carillon of York Minster bells and with a hearty send-off to Peter, Anna and Jane as they went their separate ways at the end of the Grand Départ.

I, of course, managed a few more covert detours to take photos of St Wilfrid's church, some more shop windows and to join Purple Man on his static bike art challenge on Stonegate. There were so many things still to do and so little time to do them.

Eventually, we too had to return home. We had to get back to normal life.

The transition would be aided, regrettably, by the fact that I had forgotten to press 'record' on the TV box before we left on Friday. I wasn't therefore able to immerse myself in too much more cycling that evening. I had the Sunday highlights but little to show for Saturday.

It was back to earth with a bump but with many happy memories of a job well done.

As for the race, there are many other commentators better than I who have narrated it for posterity in other more worthy publications. I won't try to distil it here, much as I would love to be able to wax lyrically about Peter Sagan's wheelie on the Côte de Wincobank and the successful lone attack by Vincenzo Nibali in the Don Valley.

Those are stories for more seasoned cycling authors than I, but I do hope that in some way my little perspective on the Tour has been of interest to you.

I shall wrap up with some anecdotes about the many churches who rang for Le Tour de France and how the dreams of a legacy came true. That, of course, takes me into the story of ringing for the inaugural 2015 Tour de Yorkshire.

I'll give you a few more leads for bell-ringing; don't forget 'Your Local Tower Needs You.'

And I'll share some photos with you, some taken by myself, some by fellow ringers all along the race route, and some kindly contributed by great folk that I bumped into on Twitter.

CHAPTER 32

FULL ITINERARY OF BELL-RINGING FOR LE TOUR

2012	
December	Yorkshire confirmed as host for the 2014 Grand Départ

2013	
January	First meeting with Welcome to Yorkshire to mention the idea of church bells
May	Bells become a common topic at Tour Roadshow events across the county
All year	'Tower Briefings' and attendance at AGMs to explain Le Tour to bell-ringers
	New band of ringers sign up at Otley especially to be able to welcome Le Tour
October	Top ten towers of Le Tour in Yorkshire submitted for media Yellow Book
December	Welcome to Yorkshire formally invite bell-ringing for the festival and for Le Tour

2014	
January	Wombel training bell features in media launch of Yorkshire Festival in Leeds
March	Oxenhope and Haworth ring to welcome BBC Tandem for Sport Relief
	BBC *Songs of Praise* 'bell-ringing for Le Tour' pre-recorded in Otley
	Ripon bells welcome dignitaries to the Tour 100-Day Dinner in the Cathedral
	Sheffield St. Marie's ring a quarter peal for first anniversary of new bells in Notre Dame
	Bell-ringing interviews on BBC Radio Leeds and York at Y14
	Australian bells live on BBC Radio Leeds for Le Tour
	BBC Radio 4 *Bells on Sunday* features Sheffield Cathedral
April	Mytholmroyd bells duet with Kathryn Stott in The Grand Departs' piano pull

	BBC Radio 4 *Bells on Sunday* features York St Wilfrid's
	Knaresborough ringers launch their 100-Day Ringing Programme ahead of Le Tour
April – July	'Bell-ringers Herald Cyclists' is one of forty-seven headline events in the Yorkshire Festival
May	Dewsbury Minster Fest lets the community try church bells and the Wombel
	Article and photos in *The Ringing World* (issue 5,376)
June	Penistone bells feature on ITV *Calendar* as the launch of the 'Big Ring'
	Tower open days in several churches
	BBC *Songs of Praise* Tour de France edition on air including bells
	BBC Radio 4 *Bells on Sunday* features Chapel Allerton
	Massive yellow jersey unveiled on the tower of Holy Trinity, Skipton
July	Bells on the big screen at the Tour de France opening ceremony
	Cawthorne, Ossett, Chapel Allerton and Masham on screen at the ceremony
	BBC *Look North* report live from Leeds Minster ringing chamber during the ceremony
	Seventy churches across the county ring for the ceremony
	York, Australia and New York, USA ring Yorkshire for Le Tour
	Sheffield Cathedral and Leeds Minster bells filmed for festival films
	Bell-ringing and open days all along the race route of Le Tour in Yorkshire
	BBC Radio 4 *Bells on Sunday* features York Minster
	Article and photos in *The Ringing World* (issue 5,387)

2015

April	BBC Radio Sheffield breakfast show interview about bells for the Tour de Yorkshire
May	BBC Radio Humberside cover Beverley & District ringing for the Tour de Yorkshire
July	Draft of this book submitted to Vertebrate Publishing on the Monday before the 2015 Tour Grand Depart. Contract signed on 26 July, the final day of the race

CHAPTER 33

THINGS I LEARNT – USEFUL TIPS IF YOU WANT TO TRY THIS YOURSELF

During the course of Le Tour de France in Yorkshire, I learnt a huge amount about my own county. I also learnt a few things about events that I hope may be useful to you if you happen to have chance to do something similar.

1. Be bold – no idea is totally stupid
2. Wear spots – suits make for dull meetings
3. Beware committees – they can waste your time
4. Trust the grass roots – you will be constantly surprised
5. Tweet and greet – Twitter beats LinkedIn
6. Take risks – comfort zones make for dull stories
7. Ride bikes – you feel sharper in body and in mind
8. Ring bells – the world likes them
9. Be patient – not everyone understands email, phones or even letters
10. Be persistent – sometimes you have to get pushy
11. Get out there – #BePartOfIt
12. Press record – if not, you'll get home and won't be able to watch the race.

CHAPTER 34

LES TOWERS DE FRANCE –
THE TOWERS OF THE RACE ROUTE

There was some debate about the number of bell towers on the race route.

We never reached a final consensus on the maximum allowable distance between the church and the bikes.

Obviously, the towers standing roadside for the race would be the key ones to engage the riders and the media on the day, but with several tons of heavy metal ready to ring out, churches a little off the main route had the potential to make an audible impact on the race and to be part of the general festivities of the day.

I list forty churches. Broadly speaking these were roadside or up a side road nearby or across a field. Pretty close. And with the exception of Holmbridge, they were all members of the Yorkshire Association of Change Ringers.

Holmbridge has just one bell and a bell-ringer. They cannot, therefore, ring changes and so would be unlikely to have ever considered trying to join an association of change ringers. However, for me, they were one of the most exciting towers of the race.

Holme is, perhaps unsurprisingly, on the ascent of Holme Moss, the Alpe d'Huez of British cycling. The church stands boldly on a sweeping chicane in a short flat between sharp steps of the climb.

Holmbridge only found out about 'The Big Ring' for the Tour opening ceremony the day before, but quicker than you could say 'pneu crevé' they pulled together the most remarkable event. I shall let them tell you about it in their own words after I share the main list of towers in the 2014 race.

STAGE ONE	Bells	Dedication	O.S. Grid Ref	Motorcade arrives	Cyclists arrive
Leeds Cathedral	8	St Anne	300 339	1000	1200
Leeds Minster	13	St Peter	306 333	1000	1200
Chapel Allerton	6	St Matthew	303 374	1003	1203
Harewood	3	All Saints	314 451	1005	1206
Otley	8	All Saints	201 454	1013	1212
Ilkley	8	All Saints	116 478	1028	1228
Addingham	6	St Peter	085 497	1036	1234
Skipton	8	Holy Trinity	991 519	1052	1249
Rylstone	3	St Peter	971 588	1105	1302
Kettlewell	3	St Mary	971 722	1128	1324
Aysgarth	6	St Andrew	012 885	1205	1359
Askrigg	6	St Oswald	948 911	1217	1411
Grinton	6	St Andrew	046 984	1310	1501
Middleham	8	St Mary & St Alkelda	126 879	1331	1521
East Witton	6	St John the Evangelist	147 860	1336	1526
Masham	10	St Mary the Virgin	227 807	1353	1541
West Tanfield	6	St Nicholas	268 788	1402	1550
Ripon Cathedral	13	St Peter & St Wilfrid	314 711	1414	1601
Harrogate	8	St Wilfrid	294 556	1444	1630
Harrogate	8	St Peter	302 554	1446	1632
Stage finish				1446	1632

STAGE TWO	Bells	Dedication	O.S. Grid Ref	Motorcade arrives	Cyclists arrive
York St Martin	8	St Martin	601 519	0920	1120
York Minster	14	St Peter	603 522	0922	1122
York St Wilfrid	10	St Wilfrid	601 521	0923	1123
Knaresborough	8	St John Baptist	347 572	0954	1152
Harrogate		See Stage One		1005	1203
Blubberhouses	3	St Andrew	167 553	1036	1232
Addingham again	6	St Peter	085 497	1050	1245
Silsden	6	St James the Great	041 465	1102	1256
Keighley	8	St Andrew	061 410	1106	1300
Haworth	6	St Michael & All Angels	030 372	1122	1316
Oxenhope	8	St Mary the Virgin	030 347	1132	1325
Heptonstall	8	St Thomas the Apostle	986 280	1146	1338
Mytholmroyd	8	St Michael	013 260	1151	1343
Ripponden	8	St Bartholomew	041 198	1217	1408
Elland	8	St Mary	108 212	1227	1418
Huddersfield	10	St Peter	146 168	1237	1427
Armitage Bridge	6	St Paul	134 137	1249	1438
Holmfirth	8	Holy Trinity	143 082	1259	1448
High Bradfield	8	St Nicholas	267 925	1401	1547
Sheffield Cathedral	13	St Peter & St Paul	354 875	Off route	
Sheffield Cathedral	8	St Marie	354 872	Off route	
Stage finish				1446	1629

CHURCH BELL TOWERS OF LE TOUR YORKSHIRE

Leeds Cathedral, St Anne's

Virtually overlooking the ceremonial start line of the Grand Départ, St Anne's is the first bell tower on the race route of Le Tour de France in Yorkshire. Its history began in 1786, growing from chapel to cathedral over the next century, but in 1899 it was compulsorily purchased by Leeds Corporation as part of the renovation of this area of the city. The new, neo-Gothic cathedral was built yards from its predecessor. It has eight bells in the key of G.

Leeds Minster, St Peter

Tantalisingly close to the race, but a few blocks south of the Grand Départ, Leeds Minster nevertheless hosted BBC *Look North* on the evening of the Tour de France opening ceremony. Grade-I listed, it meets the 1830s Vicar of Leeds' request to hold as many people as possible. With over 1,600 seats it delivers a large congregation to enjoy its thirteen bells in the key of C.

Chapel Allerton, St Matthew's,

The present church was consecrated in 1900, but old manuscripts indicate a 'Capella de Alreton' as far back as 1240. The area itself, but without a chapel, is mentioned in the Domesday Book as Alretun, 'the settlement by the alder trees'. St Matthew's re-energised these ancient French links by ringing out a short distance from the cyclists as they processed to Harewood House for the formal race start. Its six bells in B also rang out on BBC Radio 4 *Bells on Sunday* in the month before the Grand Départ.

Its ringers appeared on screen at the Tour de France opening ceremony, as one of four towers pre-filmed by ITV for broadcast during Gary Verity's welcoming speech. *With thanks to Chapel Allerton church for this photo.*

Harewood, All Saints

Harewood's three bells are largely unringable at present. However, they remain an interesting part of this fifteenth century church in the grounds of Harewood House. The church is maintained by the Churches Conservation Trust and houses a very fine collection of medieval alabaster tomb effigies. This grand old building contributed to the splendour of the Harewood Estate, as the Red Arrows flew overhead and as Royal guests cut the ribbon for the formal race start of the 2014 Tour de France. *With thanks to Steve Davey for this photo.*

Otley, All Saints

Otley was one of the great Saxon parishes surveyed in the Domesday Book, and the Anglian crosses in the baptistry have been dated at AD 750. The Norman chancel is dated 1240, the East window was inserted in 1490, and the pulpit, from which John Wesley preached, is Georgian. Otley is famous as the birthplace of Thomas Chippendale the master furniture designer, who was baptised in the church on 5 June 1781. The church has a ring of eight bells, in the key of F. Its ropes have Yorkshire tail-ends. Otley bell-ringers hosted BBC *Songs of Praise* for their Tour de France edition, filmed in March and broadcast on the Sunday before the Grand Départ. *With thanks to Otley church for this photo.*

Ilkley, All Saints

Christians have worshipped on this site since about AD 627. The church would have been built of stone taken from the abandoned Roman fort of Olicana which stood on this spot. The present building is partly medieval, but largely Victorian. As their website says, 'Each generation has adapted the building to suit its needs, but the Gospel message has remained unchanged throughout the centuries.' Ilkley is renowned for its Saxon crosses. It is also renowned as the home of Jasper Snowdon, one of the most influential figures in the development of change ringing. The church now has eight bells in the key of E. *With thanks to Ilkley church for this photo.*

Addingham, St Peter

A Grade-I listed building on high ground above the River Wharfe. There has been Christian worship on this site since the Archbishop of York took refuge there from the Viking invaders in AD 867. A later monk tells how the Archbishop, Wulfhere, found refuge at 'Hatynghame in Hwerverdale, upon the bank of the River Hwerf between Otley and the Castle of Sciptun.' The present building dates from the fifteenth century. Recent dendrochronology (timber dating) shows that the timber used in the magnificent Tudor roof was from trees felled in AD 1476–1512. The bell tower has six bells which were installed in 1759 at a cost of £246. 1s. od. Some of the bells have mottoes inscribed on them including, 'Our voices shall, with joyful sound, make hills and valleys echo round'. Addingham was honoured as the only place to feature on both Stage One and Stage Two of Le Tour. Its bells rang out for the race. *Photo courtesy of Derek Johnstone.*

Skipton, Holy Trinity

Holy Trinity church stands at the top of the High Street next to the Norman castle originally built by Robert de Romille from Brittany. The fourteenth century church has a large west tower which dominates the surrounding buildings. It contains a magnificent peal of eight bells with the heaviest bell weighing over one tonne. They rank amongst the very best in Yorkshire and indeed the world. Skipton captured the imagination of TV viewers during the race as it hosted a five-metre square yellow jersey on the church tower. Helicopters hovered over the church, broadcasting this jersey to the world. *Photo courtesy of Steve Davey.*

Rylstone, St Peter

The earliest church at 'Rilleston' was around 1160 and was probably a wooden structure. The present church, the fourth on the site, was consecrated in 1853. It has three bells, the tenor weighing seven hundredweight. One bears the inscription 'Gloria in Excelsis Deo 1648' and another, 'God Us Ayde'. The church now serves the Wharfedale communities of Rylstone, Cracoe, Hetton and Bordley in the Yorkshire Dales. *Photo courtesy of Rylstone church.*

Kettlewell, St Mary

The present church is Grade-II listed and a church has stood on this site since 1120. The tower, housing three bells, is all that remains of a previous Georgian church demolished in 1882. Inside the church stands an ancient stone font from the original Norman church. Its stained glass windows commemorate and depict the First World War and Second World War, with one signed 'William Morris 1953'. Kettlewell's three bells were not ringable for Le Tour, however, the church did reach

170

out to visitors on the day offering a quiet space for reflection. Kettlewell is also renowned for its scarecrows, many of which celebrated Le Tour. *With thanks to Kettlewell church for the photo.*

Aysgarth, St Andrews

A Grade-II listed building, overlooking the magnificent Aysgarth Falls and with reputedly the largest churchyard in England. The church was largely rebuilt in 1866 but on a site with religious origins in Saxon times. The tower base is twelfth century. The church is now detached from Aysgarth village, which has moved up the hill over the centuries. It is home to the Jervaulx Screen, brought from Jervaulx Abbey after the Dissolution of Monasteries (1538). It houses a ring of six bells in the key of F.

Askrigg, St Oswald

A mile or so off the race route, Askrigg was nevertheless a prime location for fans staying in the Dales. Askrigg's small local band of ringers are keenly seeking new recruits to enjoy their six bells in the key of G. The church dates from the fifteenth century. It includes some earlier work but was also extensively restored in the 1850s. The church is Grade-I listed. Directly facing its east window is Sykes's House, Village Store and Tearoom, with the winged wheel of the Cyclists' Touring Club above its door.

Grinton, St Andrew

St Andrew's church dates back over 900 years and stands next to an historic crossing point of the River Swale. The west tower dates from the late twelfth century and adds dignity to this large spreading church.

There are six bells including one cast in the seventeenth century. This is the largest church in Swaledale and rightly deserves its description as 'The Cathedral of the Dale'. St Andrew's sits at the foot of Grinton Moor, a dramatic climb with stunning scenery giving us some of the iconic photos of the 2014 Tour. *Photo with kind permission from John Wilkinson. Grinton is, at the time of writing, seeking new ringers and is raising money to augment its bells from six to eight.*

Middleham, St Mary and St Alkelda

Middleham church is unusual in being dedicated to two saints. Alkelda was an Anglo Saxon princess reputedly strangled by Viking invaders. A well dedicated to her name is to the north of the church. The tall west tower contains a peal of eight bells of fine tone with the heaviest bell weighing just under one tonne. Despite its size the church is, however, dwarfed by the ruins of nearby Middleham Castle, childhood home of Richard III.

East Witton, The Church of St John the Evangelist

Built between 1809 and 1813 at the instigation and expense of the Earl of Aylesbury, squire of Jervaulx. The Earl of Aylesbury's family name was Brudnel Bruce. The Bruce family coat of arms is depicted on the hatchment. Part of this coat of arms is a blue lion. When the pub in the village was refurbished in the late eighteenth/early nineteenth centuries, it was renamed The Blue Lion. Next door lived the late TV presenter Richard Whiteley (of Channel 4 *Countdown* fame) whose ashes are buried in the churchyard.

Masham, St Mary's

Masham was described in the 1820s as a parish in the wapentake of Hang East, a wapentake being a division of certain northern and midland English counties. Today Masham is much better known for its large marketplace and its twin breweries, Theakston and Black Sheep, both of which were much sampled during the summer of 2014. Pronounced Mass'em, Masham and its church have Saxon origins, but the present building is mainly Norman with fifteenth-century additions. Masham bells joined Chapel Allerton on the big screen at the Tour opening ceremony, being pre-filmed by ITV.

West Tanfield, St Nicholas

A Grade-II listed building, founded in the thirteenth century. Home to a ring of six bells, the tenor bell weighing ten hundredweight and struck in the key of G. The church contains the 'Marmion Tomb', unique in the UK and comprising

of life-size alabaster effigies. The Marmion family home is at Fontenay-au-Marmion near William the Conqueror's birthplace of Falaise in Normandy, France. William and Marmion were both descended from Rollo the Ganger, an early Duke of Normandy. Beside the church is the beautiful Marmion Tower, a fifteenth century gatehouse of a now vanished riverside manor house and former home of the Marmion family. The famous view of the church from the River Ure (as the Tour goes over the bridge) has been captured by many artists and photographers.

Ripon Cathedral, St Peter and St Wilfrid

There has been a cathedral on this site since 672 when Wilfrid first established his church here. Archbishop Roger of Pont l'Eveque began its rebuilding in the late twelfth century. By around 1230 the west front and its two towers were complete. The south tower of this pair contains a peal of twelve bells, the newest twelve in Yorkshire. In March 2014, the cathedral hosted the 100-Day Dinner for the riders and dignitaries of the race. *Photo courtesy of Sheila Webb.*

Harrogate, St Wilfrid's

St Wilfrid's is the masterpiece of Temple Moore, an eminent architect of the early 1900s. During its construction, its earliest congregations gathered in a temporary corrugated iron building known as the 'Tin Tabernacle'. Later congregations have, however, been able to worship in what has become Harrogate's only Grade-I listed building. It is also the subject of Sir John Betjeman's 'Perp Revival i' the North'. St Wilfrid's has eight bells in the key of C and opened its belfry doors for a very well-attended public open day during the build up to Le Tour. *Photo courtesy of Jonathan Wilson.*

Harrogate, St Peter's

A Victorian church right at the heart of the town, 300 metres from the finishing line of Stage One. The windows are the most interesting historical feature, all by Burlison and Grylls and put in after the First World War. The firm allowed the donors to put in photographic representations of people in whose memory the windows were given as the faces of saints. The church has an impressive peal of eight bells, a magnificent choir and a large and enthusiastic music group. St Peter's is best known for providing a daily hot breakfast for the homeless and hungry and for the food bank it has operated for over twenty-five years, giving out food parcels every evening. St Peter's bells rang out throughout the afternoon of the Grand Départ, and its ringers had a grand-stand view of the finishing straight. *Thanks to St Peter's for the photo and for many great toasted teacakes.*

York St Martin's, Coney Street

St Martin's welcomed Tour fans to join them for a Tower Open Day on Sunday 6 July. Coney Street was packed with fans, the church was packed with cakes and the ringers had a privileged view down on to proceedings. The church, with eight bells in G#, dates from the eleventh century and is famous for its clock overhanging York's main shopping street. It has been restored following severe bomb damage in the Second World War.

York Minster, St Peter

Completed in 1472, York Minster is one of the largest Gothic cathedrals in Northern Europe. In the twelfth century Roger Pont l'Eveque was responsible for its rebuilding after a fire. The east window has the largest expanse of medieval stained glass in the world. No less impressive are the bells, a peal of twelve bells with the heaviest weighing three tonnes, an equally heavy clock chime of six bells, a bourdon bell, Great Peter, of nearly eleven tonnes and a carillon of thirty-six bells – the only carillon in an English cathedral. The ringers at York Minster rang a quarter peal on the morning of Stage Two. Their ringers had a bird's eye view of the ceremonial procession through the city.

York, St Wilfrid's

St Wilfrid's was very active around Le Tour, including 'Le Grand Weekend' on 5 and 6 July. Its gardens hosted hundreds of visitors for tea, cakes and strawberries; its carved stone tympanum over its doorway was enriched with Tour bunting and fans on the pavement outside had one of the best viewpoints in the city, with York Minster just along the road. The current Roman Catholic church was completed in 1864 in the Gothic revival style. Its tower stands 147 feet tall and houses a fine ring of ten bells in the key of F.

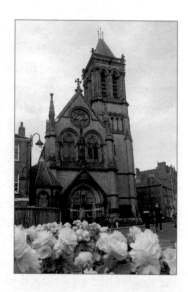

Knaresborough, St John the Baptist

St John's dates from 1114 when King Henry I gave the church to the Augustinian Priory at Nostell. It stands high above the steep-sided valley of the River Nidd. Higher still than the church are the remains

of Knaresborough Castle where the murderers of Thomas à Beckett once took refuge. The central tower of the medieval church, with its needle spire, contains a peal of eight bells many of which date back to the eighteenth century. St John's is a beautiful and ancient parish church but it is not just a nostalgic reminder of ancient Christian England. It has a living, vibrant and committed worshipping congregation. People have worshipped in this building for nearly 1,000 years. *Photo courtesy of Viv Graham.*

Blubberhouses, St Andrew

The church dates from the 1850s when Lady Frankland Russell, of Blubberhouses Hall, decided to build a chapel of ease so that her estate workers could worship without having to walk to Fewston. Her architect, Edward Buckton Lamb, was known as the 'Rogue Architect' because he believed in the architectural style known as true Gothic. The church, with its three bells, looks down on to a road known in July 2014 as the Côte de Blubberhouses, an early part of the second stage of Le Tour. *Photo courtesy of Derek Johnstone.*

Silsden, St James

Silsden church dates from 1711, being built when the village was much smaller and when its inhabitants faced challenging journeys on bridle paths to get to the nearest other churches. It is dedicated to St James the Fisherman, son of Zebedee and Salome. In common with the famous pilgrimage route across northern Spain to Santiago de Compostela, it hosts a number of St James scallop shells, carved into woodwork around the church. Silsden's six bells in the key of A rang out for the race. Great views of the race were had from the church as it looked down on to the sweeping road through the village. *Photo courtesy of Derek Johnstone.*

Keighley, St Andrew

The earliest records of Christianity in Keighley are not of a church, but of a ninth century graveyard and Anglian cross shaft where visiting monks may have preached. The earliest charter for a church is dated 1168, the church of St Andrew of Kichalaie. Over the years the Kyghelays married into the Cavendish family and the current church was built in Victorian times. It boasts eight bells in the key of F. *With thanks to Cherry Connolly for the photo.*

Haworth, St Michael and All Angels

World famous for being the home of the Brontë family, Haworth parsonage stands behind St Michael and All Angels church. The present church dates from the late nineteenth century with just the lower part of the tower remaining from the earlier church. The peal of six bells, however, predates the rebuilding and would have been the very bells which called the Brontës to worship. *Photo received via Jane Hedley of the Yorkshire Historic Churches Trust.*

Oxenhope, St Mary the Virgin

With eight bells in F#, Oxenhope was well-tuned into Le Tour. Its ringers rang for the BBC Tandem Team in the spring and for the big weekend itself in July. Its churchyard was bedecked with bunting. Architects' drawings of the church date from 1849. In 1845, Reverend Patrick Brontë, father of the novelist sisters, appointed the curate Reverend Joseph Brett Grant to take charge of the new parish. Services began in a wool combing shop, a day school was built and eventually the church. Its early Norman style gives the impression of a much older church. *Photo courtesy of Derek Johnstone.*

Heptonstall, St Thomas the Apostle

The original church was dedicated to St Thomas à Becket in 1260 but following severe storms a new church was built in 1854. Much of its stone was quarried on the site itself. The church has three churchyards, the newest of which is where Sylvia Plath, American poet and first wife of former poet laureate, Ted Hughes, is buried. Heptonstall has eight bells in the key of E. Its bells rang out in Tour week and the church looked across fields to the race as it descended into Hebden Bridge. *Photo courtesy of Derek Johnstone.*

Mytholmroyd, St Michael's

The church tower looked out over The Grand Departs' piano pull, in which eighteen bikes were bolted together to pull a grand piano up Cragg Vale. St Michael's has eight bells in the key of F. It was built in 1847 as a 'Million Pound Church', under an Act to build churches in industrial areas for middle and lower classes. The fund of money for these churches came from indemnities paid to Britain by Austria following the Napoleonic Wars. Mytholmroyd derives its name from Mithomrode, a clearing where two rivers meet. In 2014 it was the venue for the world's top cyclists meeting the longest continuous incline in England, Cragg Vale.

Ripponden, St Bartholomew

St Bart's is sited at the foot of the Category-3 Côte de Ripponden on stage two of Le Tour. It hosted colourful flower displays in the build-up to the race and its eight bells in G rang out on the morning ahead of the race. The first church was consecrated in 1464, prior to which worshippers had a long trek to Elland. Floods damaged a replacement church in 1722, with bodies washed from graves and a coffin caught up a tree. The present church is the fourth in the valley and has fine stained glass windows. *Photo courtesy of Jean Doman. Taken during a ringing trip.*

Elland, St Mary the Virgin

A Grade-I listed stone church built around 1180 on a high plateau overlooking the River Calder and canal. Long reaching views available from the top of the tower along the valley floor and hilltops. Sir John Savile's family badge, an owl was added in the thirteenth century on two of the buttresses. The large east window has magnificent medieval glass and is said to be one of the finest in Yorkshire. The tower built in the fifteenth century has four large clock faces. Home to eight bells cast by William Dobson's, Downham Market in 1826. The nearby cricket ground was a busy campsite when Le Tour came to Calderdale. *Photo courtesy of Peter Uttley.*

Huddersfield, St Peter

With its tall tower and ten bells in E♭, St Peter's stands boldly watching over the comings and goings in Huddersfield town centre. A parish church has stood there for 1,000 years, the first being built by Walter de Laci as a promise after being thrown from his horse into a swampy marsh en route from Halifax to Huddersfield. Fearing for his life, he vowed that if he were spared, he would found a church in Huddersfield. It was built around 1090–1100, the earlier Domesday Book of 1085 recording no church in Odersfelt. It is a few years since I have rung there, but I recall the ringers being rare in having a kettle up the tower to warm their band with a much needed cuppa on cold practice nights. *Photo courtesy of Huddersfield church.*

Armitage Bridge, St Paul

St Paul's rang heartily with towers across Yorkshire on the evening of the Tour opening ceremony and the church was a very busy refreshment centre on race day. Its ringers hosted their finest deckchairs roadside for spectacular views of the Tour riders as the race came through the community on 6 July. The church was originally built in 1848 thanks to the Brooke Family. It suffered a devastating fire more recently though and was rebuilt in 1987.

Holmfirth, Holy Trinity

Holmfirth tower looks across the River Holme to the race route of Le Tour. The courtyard at its side accommodates Sid's Café, much loved from *Last of Summer Wine* and a fine venue for tea and cake on a bike ride in this magnificent corner of Yorkshire. With tightly packed woollen mill cottages around it, Holmfirth's bells call out to the community for new ringers. On race day, they were kindly helped by the ringers of New Mill. A year later, New Mill rang from their own tower, close to the route of the inaugural 2015 Tour de Yorkshire.

Bradfield, St Nicholas

A Grade-I listed building, founded in the early fifteenth century. An idyllic setting, with sheep grazing in the churchyard during the late spring and summer months. The west tower has a fine peal of eight bells in F, which sound out over the moors and dales of the Peak District National Park. The church includes an altar with an ancient French Reredos and a modern memorial to the Sheffield flood of 1864. The church has an unusual watchhouse at the gates, still lived in by the church verger, and built during the eighteenth century to watch over the churchyard and prevent grave robberies. Nearby is the ancient manmade mound of the 'Bailey Hill' and a ninth-century Anglo Saxon cross.

Sheffield Cathedral, St Peter and St Paul

Formerly the Parish Church of Sheffield, it gained cathedral status in 1914. The bells rang out on the afternoon of the Tour opening ceremony. Its ringers were filmed as part of the summary films for the 2014 Yorkshire Festival and the ringing coincided with two headline Festival acts downstairs – the Festival of Colour, Space and Light and the hosting of all ten knitted bikes from the Woolly Bikes community project. The cathedral houses thirteen bells in C# and has origins a thousand years old.

Sheffield Cathedral, St Marie (RC)

St Marie's is somewhat newer, having been completed in 1850. Prior to the Protestant reformation, its congregation would have worshipped at St Peter & Paul, but it was not until the early 1800s that Catholic churches were rebuilt. St Marie's is renowned for its tall tower. Its eight bells in the key of D have marked many occasions. During the build-up to Le Tour, its band rang a quarter peal to celebrate the first anniversary of the installation of new bells at Notre Dame in Paris.

CHURCHES THAT RANG FOR THE OPENING CEREMONY OF LE TOUR

Holmbridge, Holme Moss	Cottingham	Meltham
Mirfield	Hessle	Thornton in Craven
Leathley	Burstwick	Easingwold
Darfield	Elloughton	Acomb
Fewston	Middleton on the Wolds	Rufforth
Aldborough	Nafferton	Leeds St Annes
Boroughbridge	Far Headingley	Leeds Minster
Northallerton	Pontefract All Saints	Chapel Allerton
Almondbury	Rothwell	Otley
Marsden	Barwick in Elmet	Addingham
Tong	Kirk Deighton	Masham
Richmond	Filey	Harrogate St Peter
Northowram	Flamborough	York St Wilfrid
Kirkthorpe	Brompton by Sawdon	Silsden
Woolley	Wykeham	Haworth
Hightown, Castleford	Selby Abbey	Heptonstall
Whitby	Wetherby	Armitage Bridge
Ormesby	Saxton	High Bradfield
Hurworth	South Anston	Dewsbury Minster
Kirkby Malzeard	Wortley	Penistone
Kirklington	Mexborough	Cawthorne
Sowerby	Giggleswick	Ossett
Longwood	Idle	

Churches 'overseas' that also joined in the big ring to welcome Le Tour: Whickham, Hampshire; Bournemouth, Dorset.

And so, after sharing stories of the 'change ringing' churches on the race route, here, as promised, is the story of St David's Holmbridge. Thanks to Sandy Wise for the write up which follows.

Located on a tight bend at the very foot of the Holme Moss climb, the church, cricket club and pub of Holmbridge were well-placed to join together to provide hospitality to visitors and locals alike.

A last minute comment in an email from Welcome to Yorkshire, mentioned something about bells ringing on the Thursday evening at the end of the Welcome Ceremony in Leeds. This led one of St David's congregation to investigate further and make contact with Rod Ismay. Although we soon found that Rod's plans were based around churches with full peals, we didn't want to miss out.

With minutes to go, there were just a handful of people, but a crowd appeared from all corners, including the local scout troop, fully uniformed and on bikes, all with bells. So at the appointed hour, the church bell was joined by bikes and bells, grannies with cowbells, teachers with school bells all making a joyful noise (or deafening racket depending on your viewpoint). The kids' favourite was a very old handbell without a clapper, which when hit with a wooden spoon, literally left your ears ringing. Cyclists on their way up Holme Moss, dog walkers and even the bus stopped to see what was going on. Two minutes ringing, then it was all over and we dispersed for bike rides, to the pub or over to the cricket field for a run around. It was a fun and fitting way to begin the festivities for Le Tour.

For the weekend itself, St David's provided many visitors with a welcome repose from the crowds and sustenance for the soul in a wonderful labyrinth – an exhibition that reflected on the journey of life. We also offered hospitality in the way of indoor camping and breakfasts in the hall, parking for campervans and cars and the usual best of English church tea and cake in the church itself.

> *Holmbridge Cricket club provided beer and hog-roasts as well as a large screen to watch as the race continued up over Holme Moss into Derbyshire. The Bridge Pub also had live music all weekend and a viewing platform.*
>
> *When to ring the bell? Tour Makers told us to watch for the red official car followed by gendarmes, so the bell was rung again, welcomed by a loud cheer from the assembled crowd. The noise of helicopters overhead signalled they were here and the bell-ringer rushed out just in time to see the leader …*
>
> *What a weekend, a great community event. We raised nearly £2,000 for some urgent tower repairs and a donation to our partner charity, the Memusi Foundation.*

Some communities even built their own towers for Le Tour.

Burley-in-Wharfedale Scouts and Guides took it upon themselves to build a seven-metre replica Eiffel Tower. The tower was built as part of a fundraising project for a new 'community use building' for the Scouts and Guides headquarters. It attracted much media interest. Donations can still be made by typing 'Burley Scouts and Guides' on the Virgin Giving charities page.

When the Tour had passed, the tower was put up for sale on eBay:

> *For Sale: Eiffel Tower – buyer to collect. Are you an old romantic at heart, but can't be bothered to go to Paris? Maybe your own back garden lacks the sort of iconic landmark you feel it really needs? If you are looking for an Eiffel Tower for a party or wedding reception, we have just the thing for you. Offers, welcome. Oh – and you'll need a big truck.*

Bids were indeed received for the tower, but sadly the winning bidder then failed to materialise with the money. Otley Masonic Lodge heard of the hoax bid and kindly donated the bid price of £350, a wonderful gesture for the Scouts. The tower itself met its end on Bonfire Night.

CHAPTER 35

TOUR DE YORKSHIRE 2015

In the months before the 2014 Grand Départ, Welcome to Yorkshire had begun to talk of an annual Tour de Yorkshire, a pro-cycling race to build on the passion that was so evident in the build-up to Le Tour. Respected commentators in other countries were, in all seriousness, talking of Yorkshire as the new world capital of cycling. The fans and riders, meanwhile, were in no doubt that the county's mixture of tough terrain, magnificent scenery and knowledgeable crowds was a potent combination for a recurring fixture.

Where bikes go, bells go, so I was soon tweeting suggestions for the 2015 race route and then plotting out the towers when the stage maps were formally announced during the winter.

By this time, my life outside of work was dominated by writing this book. Thankfully though it would be a little easier to organise the ringing in 2015 for three reasons. Firstly, bells were firmly established in the psyche of the race. Secondly, we had the templates and experience from 2014 which we could unleash and edit for ease in 2015. And lastly and most importantly the ringers of East Yorkshire were chomping at the bit for a piece of the action. They had narrowly missed out on hosting part of the Grand Départ but were determined not to miss out second time round.

The Beverley & District Society of Change Ringers were straight out of the blocks with an inspiring programme of ringing performances, public open days and radio interviews. So too were the Selby & District Branch, Scarborough & District Branch, Central Branch and Western Branch. This thing had some momentum now.

The May Day bank holiday weekend saw a fantastic three days' racing starting in Bridlington on the Friday. Bells rang out along the route, but year-end meetings at work meant I could only watch on Twitter for Stage One. For Stages Two and Three, however, I had active plans to make a noise.

Holme on Spalding Moor has a fabulous church on a dramatic hilltop looking down to the Yorkshire Wolds. Their ringers kindly welcomed me to join them in a pre-race ring, for Stage Two, before we tailed the Giant Alpecin and Cofidis team cars north to Norton on Derwent, them scouting out the roads, us looking for church towers. We sounded out a joyful welcome across the town and then drove the race route in reverse to see how the ringers had got on at Wetwang. I would have loved to have rung at all these places. Does anyone have a helicopter that they can lend us for next year, to get us around?

The most emotional day though was Stage Three in Barnsley. There, the riders took a sweeping right turn past the magnificent town hall, wove left up cobblestones on Church Street and then accelerated towards the hills and a reverse ride along the roads of Stage Two from the 2014 Tour. The emotional part was getting closure on our unfinished business from Bradfield and staying focused for a fifty-minute quarter peal as the bands played outside, as the police motorbike sirens screamed past and as the crowds roared at the approach of the riders. This was 'hairs on neck' time. This was slight 'tear in the eye' time. And it was almost disaster when I left the tower door unlocked and some keen visitors tried to open the ringing chamber door, nearly pushing two ringers over. Sorry. Please come again. We would love you to ring with us. Sorry that we just had to finish our quarter peal that day, which we duly did. It wasn't the 'unrung method' from Bradfield but it was a formal and hard-earned performance for the bike race.

At the same time as getting the bells ringing for the bikes again, we also got into the saddle once more on the fundraising front. This time, it was for the Tour de Yorkshire's 2015 charity partner, Sheffield Children's Hospital.

Living in Sheffield, as we did, this was an institution which we had some personal experience of, which had been a godsend to many of our friends and which we knew would resonate with the congregation of Ecclesall Church. Oh yes, here was Cycle to Church Sunday II.

We got the builder's cling-film out again, cleared the front of church for the bikes and then opened our curtains in dismay to a grey, wet Sunday, more ominous even than the invisible sunrise on Stage Two of Le Tour, a year earlier.

The rain did slacken off though and eighty riders bravely overcame the chilly breeze. Inside the church, the gift aid envelopes stayed dry, receiving kind donations which compared well to our efforts of the previous year.

Bikes are now more common at church. I'm not talking big numbers but you do see a bike by the door much more frequently now. And thus, from this embryonic cycling festival, we gave a little send off to local riders, The Fat Lads From Dore, who went on to raise many thousands more for the Children's Hospital with a challenging ride from London to Paris.

Their 'team coach' James Hope-Gill gave an inspiring talk in church, bringing to life the work of the hospital. His increasingly thin 'fat' colleagues then had a few more weeks training before riding into Paris on the day before the 2015 Tour hit the Champs-Élysées. This, then, was a fitting conclusion to two and a half years of bells and bikes.

It was an end, but also a beginning. An end of a beginning as they say. The next chapter might be over to you.

There *is* a church near you.

There *will* be a bike race near you.

I have some ideas for future Tours de Yorkshire. It'd be great to hear yours.

CHAPTER 36

ARTISTS WHO INSPIRED ME ALONG THE WAY

I am indebted to many great artists who inspired me throughout this long journey; artists whose work celebrated cycling and Yorkshireness. In the main I bumped into them on Twitter, but in some cases we went on to meet face-to-face in the real world too.

These artists covered a variety of genres from music to film, from crochet to land art and from poetry to ukulele. I am particularly grateful to two special contributors who have been invaluable in the delivery of this book.

Firstly, Jane O'Neill of Abundant Glass whose glasswork and prints of mill cottages, churches and matchstick cyclists so embodied, in the space of a beermat, the essence of Yorkshire's welcome to the race. Jane has very kindly allowed me to use one of her works for the cover of this book.

Jane's passion for cycling began around the Millennium. She has rapidly progressed from spinning pedals on an ill-fitting, poorly geared mountain bike to now riding a Bob Jackson tourer over true Tour and Giro climbs in the Alps, Pyrenees and Dolomites. With such a passion for cycling and glassmaking, it didn't take long from hearing about Yorkshire's Grand Départ to starting making glass cyclists. Jane's signature designs evolved over the spring of 2013. Her work became popular in a number of galleries and led, on 22 June 2014, to an edition of BBC *Countryfile* being broadcast from her studio with John Craven in residence. Jane's work has continued to build on her original and engaging style, with new ranges released in 2015 for the inaugural Tour de Yorkshire and for Eroica Britannia, the vintage cycle festival in the Peak District.

I am also delighted to have met and worked with Sandie Nicholson of Holmfirth Photo whose tweet of polka dot sheep was one of the earliest leftfield images to grab my attention back in December 2013. Her work has featured extensively on television. Sandie has been invited to take her camera into the heart of pro cycling in Yorkshire more than once during 2014 and 2015.

Sandie's journey began when she submitted a photo of her dog, Crumble, to ITV *Calendar*. 'Crumble in the Mist' featured on the following day's weather news and neither of them have looked back since. Sandie held key roles in the Le Tour Holmfirth Committee and in Honley Business Association. These led, amongst other things, to a highly acclaimed 'Abbey Road' style Tour pedestrian crossing and to being the featured photographer for cutover images into commercial breaks during ITV Cycling's coverage of Le Tour in Yorkshire. Sandie has subsequently been invited on to official race motorbikes with her camera and was honoured with a VIP parking permit at the Fleece Inn on Holme Moss on Stage Two.

I like their work very much. I hope you do too. Please do look them up on the internet using a search engine of your choice.

CHAPTER 37

FINDING A CHURCH NEAR YOU, WHERE YOU CAN LEARN TO RING

There are over 5,000 churches with bells hung for 'change ringing' in the UK. Most of these will ring for Sunday services and will have a practice night one day during the week.

You will typically be welcomed as a surprise guest at most churches but, with holidays and occasional special events to practise for, it is often best to get in touch with the tower correspondent beforehand to ensure that your visit will be a success.

Practice nights are generally from 7.30–9 p.m. Learners may often be welcomed to have some dedicated tuition ahead of the main practice and will then be coached at intervals during the rest of the evening. They will also have the chance to observe and learn from the 'rope skills' and 'rope sight' of more experienced ringers.

The evening may well conclude with a trip to the pub. You will soon identify who is best placed to advise on the local beverages and who understands the etiquette of gratefully being offered a drink as well as kindly offering to buy a drink …

Most counties have local associations of change ringers who will have dedicated websites upon which you may find lists of towers, their practice nights, details of tower contacts and sometimes photographs, maps and recent news from the individual churches.

Your first port call, without being in any way biased should, of course, be Yorkshire.

Equally if you type in 'bell-ringing in [some other county name]' then you are likely to find your local association high up the Google chart, or some fabulous YouTube footage by a member of that association. That in itself may be a positive aid to your tower selection.

You don't need to bring anything, the bells are there. You would be a rare, but popular individual, if you have bells in your house. (NB It is not unknown for a small number of particularly enthusiastic bell-ringers to install sets of bells in their garages or spare rooms).

You don't need to be strong. There are bells of various weights and the wheels on them are scaled to help give you the 'leverage' to turn them. I appreciate 'leverage' is not the correct mechanical term for a wheel, but I hope you get the idea.

All you need to do is turn up, have an open mind and a willingness to have a go.

Please do send me a tweet to let me know how you get on.

ACKNOWLEDGEMENTS

Massive thanks to the members of the Yorkshire Association of Change Ringers for delivering a soundtrack for Le Tour. In particular, may I thank:

My wife Sally for lovingly enduring two years of typing at 2 a.m. Our son Thomas for staying calm every time we stop to photograph a church or yellow bike. Derek and Ronalda Johnstone, wonderfully bonkers about bells and bikes and festivals. Matthew Sorrell, Australian bell-ringer, for ringing on BBC Leeds from 9,000 miles away. Rosalind Martin for my website. Helen Brankin for making Cycle to Church Sunday possible, and '20th Sheffield Scouts (Ecclesall Church)' and 'Ecclesall District Guides' for stewarding and guarding our bike park. BBC *Songs of Praise*, ITV *Calendar*, BBC *Look North* and BBC Radios Leeds, York & Sheffield for so much airtime. And Michael Orme for profiling Yorkshire in BBC Radio 4 *Bells on Sunday*. Thanks to Sharon le Corre, whose world record bunting project always gave me encouragement, and the many artists and photographers I have met on Twitter. And Vertebrate Publishing for believing in this book.

Merci beaucoup Sir Gary Verity, Welcome to Yorkshire, Martin Green and the ASO for embracing bell-ringing in such a wonderful way. Particular thanks to the Yorkshire Festival team led by David Lascelles, Henri Duckworth and Mark Fielding, and to Dee Marshall, Jenny Rose, Natalie Tam, Matthew Burgess and Anita Morris Associates for matchmaking bells with the world's media.

The caravan of Le Tour may have moved on, but Yorkshire has its own ASO pro-cycling race in the calendar now. Wherever you go along the Tour route, the yellow bikes, the church towers and the community passion are all still there.

Perhaps you might like to join us to ring for the next race. You know where we are. It's that great big tower just over there ...